Silenced Praise

You Can't Take My Voice Away

STELLA RYLAND

WESTBOW
PRESS®
A DIVISION OF THOMAS NELSON
& ZONDERVAN

WestBow Press books may be ordered through booksellers or by contacting:

WestBow Press
A Division of Thomas Nelson & Zondervan
1663 Liberty Drive
Bloomington, IN 47403
www.westbowpress.com
1 (866) 928-1240

ISBN: 978-1-9736-3613-7 (sc)
ISBN: 978-1-9736-3612-0 (e)

Print information available on the last page.

WestBow Press rev. date: 08/23/2018

CONTENTS

The word of God in Malachi 2v 12-16(NIV) states very well that the Lord was there as witness when a man married a wife of his youth, he witnessed the union between man and woman at that time. He is also saying how disappointed he is in the fact that the very same man is now neglecting and abusing the wife of his youth. If people are involved in a magnificent and beautiful wedding ceremony as guests and even as witnesses, it is the duty of the matrimonial couple to remember and acknowledge the presence of the Holy Spirit there. Which means God is present and as the author and finisher of life and faith, he is at the beginning of that marriage and will forever be present in it. The reason for me to write this book was to help someone who might be in the situation or even living the life very similar to what I wrote about in the following chapters. Some of the parts in this book are made to seem real and some are a very close fiction to reality, I can call it fantasy brought to life and emotions filled in a telling which at the end of the day will teach someone in a similar situation to rethink and maybe save her life or even prevent a very disastrous thing from happening to their life.

Our musical story takes us on a roller coaster ride of feelings such as love, pain, confusion, disappointment, forgiveness and at the end everything we see music conquering and bringing victory to those who were been oppressed and the battle been won by the same voice which is violated.

The oppressed voice rises and takes the bully to his place. A young man and woman falls in love and make promises to each other which are to be fulfilled in the future. They are both from a Christian background and are kept by this believe until they get married and a man grows his dream of becoming a music producer. The fulfilment of his dream drives him so mad to a point where he forgets the promises he made to his young love while they were busy building their life together. His promises get swallowed by the big city life, music industry and it's fame and fortune to a point where he is transformed into a beast who not only abuses his wife, he tears her apart until she has nothing and is broken down to a homeless single mother who is estranged by her husband and now to support her children she had to sink to the lowest level of humility, life takes her and throws her to the deepest sea of poverty. She is broken and humiliated by the one person who promised her the moon and the stars, the very person she trusted with her life and heart, but broken as she was and in all her predicament, there is a gift which god bestowed on her which her husband even if he tried very hard, he failed to break that. Her voice, the most beautiful and as sweet as it used to be when she was young. When life throws her lemons, she finds an opportunity to use them and make the sweetest lemonade which she could have done while in her marriage but was not given the chance to. The same voice which her husband tried to supress in their long and hard marriage, is the one which God uses not only to save a business and puts it back on a map but she get an opportunity to use that voice to become somebody well-known and respected again. The taste of fame as a gospel musician is brought to her life by a total stranger who hired her as domestic worker and discovers her while cleaning and singing. The stranger and his wife find in her what their company was missing to get back on the map and she gets an opportunity to do what she was born to do and what she was promised to by her young love who promised her the life of a star gospel musician but as soon as he got established as a music producer, he completely forgot his young promises to her. He turned her into a baby making, punching bag and ended throwing her out on the streets of a big city with their four young children. She ends reaching her dream by help from a down and out music producer whose record label was at the brink of bankruptcy. The woman not only rises from dust to stardom but she saves the company too. The same promise that her husband failed to fulfil gets established by another. The music producer who discovers the silenced praise, polishes and exposes it to the world is none other than the rival to our main character and at the end the man sees how wrong it was to suppress his wife's talent and when the role changes he tries to justify his actions but for the very first time in many years he discovers that her wife has a voice to speak up against her abuser.

Silenced praise is dedicated to all those abused women who have their dreams crushed by animals called husbands. The best way to beat a bully is by taking a stand against him. A man might be stronger that a woman but by wisdom she can win the battle against all odds. Forgiveness does not mean going back to a lying cheating good for nothing person who thinks he owns you. Nobody has the power over anyone no matter how much they pay as a bride price as the word of God clearly say that in genesis 1v26" (NIV) man and woman shall have dominion over creation" but when he made a woman out of the rib of a man he took a rib because a rib is a part of the body which protects the heart. So when the rib is broken, the heart is the first organ to feel the pain. The word of God clearly states in 1 Corinthians 13 v 4 (NLT) that "love is patient and kind, love is not jealous, boastful or proud" so my look on things is; if someone says he or she loves you, there should be nothing that causes him or her to hurt you in any way or form. If you love something which does not even have emotions or feelings, you go to every length to protect and care for it, why is it different with a human being? When God created man he saw that his image was necessary on the earth, he also noticed that man was going to be lonely in this world which was why he brought him to a deep sleep and out of his rib he made him a woman. As a person I often ask myself why God didn't take any body part but he took the rib? Why did God not use a hand? For a woman to be a helping hand or why not even a leg? The questions are many but who knows the wisdom of God except himself, after all he says he knew us before the foundations of the earth. All life has taught me is that when man says "I love this woman" that should be enough to encourage him to protect her at all costs and to prevent her from any harm especially coming from the outside. Be that as it may, no one has the right to hurt anybody man or woman. I often ask myself why when God realised that Eve convinced Adam to sin, at that time didn't separate them because it was just the two of them? As a person I sometimes wonder why he at that time not just said they went against my word so it meant that they were a bad combination and made sure that they never multiply. Yet he bless them and continued to give them life even though he made things a little difficult for them but he gave them a second chance and that was because God is love and as he gave woman to man he believed that no matter what happened nothing could separate what he had seen as a good thing. God sees a relationship of a man and woman as a very good thing and he believed that because he did not name a woman but because of the love the man saw when looking at someone who was formed from his body, he called her woman. Did God tell man that I made you sleep and removed your rib to form this one for you? I don't think so. We only read in the bible that when man woke up, he saw and named her woman without God's assistance. I call that love. It is a job of a man to see himself in his wife and if that is the case then no harm will befall her. He will at all cost protect and care for her. In the same regard as a woman when a man truly loves and protects her, she will automatically humble and submit to him but we must not blur the lines between submission and fear. If as a person you are insulted, belittled and humiliated, will you submit? No! Never. If no one is abusing the other I believe there will forever be harmony, but if someone is feared and unfairly revered then even the children of that loveless marriage are what we call damaged. In a relationship between a man and a woman the rules should be give and take not otherwise. No one is supposed to be subjected to slavery in the name of love and no one is better than the other at the end of the day God is our creator and he knows best. We both have the right to expression and as a woman you were made from man but that does not give him the right to crush down your self-esteem and dignity as a human being. No one must take away your speaking nor signing voice. Hence the book says {silenced praise} you can't take my voice away.

One

The pastor made an announcement that there was someone who was going to render an item at that service. As the congregation awaits, from the front row stood a very tiny looking girl. Her grandmother signed with her hand that she should sit down but it was already late, she was at the front and looking very confident as she greeted everyone. It was a complete shock as nobody saw that one coming. She was only twelve but due to hardships experienced through her life she looked younger than her age. No one knew that she could sing, only her grandmother but she never thought of her being confident enough to sing in front of a crowd. She knew her to be a very quiet child.

All she was known for was people would give their old clothes to her as she used to come to church with torn and very bad looking clothes. Every church member knew her as the little girl who used to carry her granny's bible bag and people knew that whenever you see her granny, it meant she was near. She would come to church every Sunday and sit at the very front row and would not move until the sermon was finished. The pastor knew her to be that little girl who would listen very attentively in church. What they did not know was she had a hidden talent, she could sing like an angel. She attended children's church but as she was very withdrawn even her teacher never knew that she could sing. When she stood there even the pastor was surprised as he only received a note saying someone was to render a musical item. The little girl took her position as she was taught by her music teacher at school. She started to breathe in and out and people thought that maybe she was nervous, little did they know that she was preparing herself.

The girl opened her mouth to sing, and what came out was shockingly amazing. She sang at the top of her voice and everyone in the church was very quiet as if somebody instructed them to be. Her granny was also so shocked at what she just saw and heard. She sang so well that when she finished, the whole congregation stood and clapped like never before. Tears rolled from her grandmother' eyes; she was so proud of her. The standing ovation made her to recognise that she just sang beautifully. It was like a butterfly just got out of the cocoon, she just saw herself do an amazing thing and everyone was approving and appreciating what she just did. That day the sermon became very different from other sermons.

From that day on little Mosa became the talk on everyone's lips. From that time at least she gained the respect even of those who went to Sunday school with her. The pastor even suggested to her grandmother that she should join a church choir which was unusual because only teenagers and youth were allowed to join the choir. Mosa's granny agreed and in no time she was not only a choir member, but she was a lead singer. That was not the only thing, as she used to sit in front always the pastor decided it was time for her to start reading the Setswana bible. She was very fluent in reading

Setswana language. That is how Mosa grew and became a respected member of the congregation. Her granny was so proud that a simple girl has just become even a role model to her peers.

She continued to impress everybody with her humble and God-fearing behaviour that the congregation decided to throw her a thirteenth birthday party. That she and her granny never ever dreamt was possible in many years. They were very grateful for what the congregation decided to do. All that was the pastor's wife's handy works. She grew very fond of Mosa as time was passing and she would even make beautiful dresses for her. She would watch and advise Mosa with her behaviour as a young girl, make sure that she had books to help her studies go smooth and even made sure that the family had food and other necessities at all times.

When she was in standard nine the pastor's wife passed away and that was heart breaking and confusing for her. She took the lady as her mother and her death really hit her hard. She had a very close relationship with her and her sudden death brought a lot of emotions to Mosa as she had a lot of questions and no one could answer. She was in a lot of pain and people were grieving their loss so no one noticed how broken she was. Everybody was focusing on their own grieve but because she was just a child, no one realised her trauma and heartbreak. She had no one to talk to and that made her very sad and lonely.

She fell into a depression state where she locked herself in her room and would not come out. She did not eat, speak to anyone or even bath for that matter. She stayed in bed and all she did was cry. All this was very difficult on her granny as Mosa's biological mother was a deadbeat. She was married to this abusive husband who kept her away from her mother and children. They lived about thirty minutes' walk from MmaLeuba's house. She did not visit them not even when one of Mosa' sibling is sick. Mmaleuba would call her, but the heartless husband would forbid her from going. The matter was so frustrating for Mosa and her siblings as they saw how their granny was struggling to maintain them. At that time the poor old lady was thinking that if Mosa's mother was around maybe she could help talk to her and comfort her out of the depressing state she was in. Mmaleuba got even more worried when Mosa stayed home in her room and not went to school for two weeks. She decided to call for help. She sent Rose (Mosa's sister who was born after her) to run and call Brother David from church. He was like an elder brother to the children in church; he also used to help as a choir master when the choir master was absent. The old lady had no choice but to call him, hoping that he will help since he is even a church counsellor.

He came and Mosa let him come into her room, they spoke for a very long time and whatever they spoke about helped because Mosa came out of her room, took a bath and asked for food. She ate and even apologised to her granny for stressing her out with her behaviour. They were so happy to see her out and about, she even went back to school the next day and the principal was also pleased to see her because she had received a message that she was not well. The principal immediately ordered her class teachers to help her catch up. She was back on track and even passed her studies that year with an A of course because that was just how clever she was. The financial trouble at home and the absent mother did not become an obstacle on her path. She went past the pain and loss to a great achievement where she entered her matric year with pride and confidence. A year after that she passed her matric and her granny gave thanks to God that at least unlike her peers in the village Mosa got her matric certificate regardless her circumstances. In that village it was a normality that a young girl at her prime should either drop out of school pregnant or she would just stay and become useless. Mosa was the only one who through all the hardships persevered and got her matric. The girls did not last in school because the villagers lived under very poor conditions but the matter was made worse by them having fatherless children. Mmaleuba was so proud of her granddaughter, she did not care or even worry about her staying home without university money or even a job; all she was excited about was the fact that unlike others Mosa has passed her matric. Mosa was also grateful that through poverty and hardship she went to school for eleven years and completed them gracefully. Why eleven? You might ask. Mosa was a very bright and brilliant child growing up, and in those days if you were found to be what is called an A student and after observation you would go to two classes in one year. That was called promotion. In Mosa's case it happened to her that she studied standard one from January to June and after winter holidays she got promoted to standard two and she passed them both brilliantly that led to her passing her matric earlier than those who started schooling in the same year with her. She was sixteen when she completed her matric, she did not even have an identity document as at that time you only qualified to have an identity document by the age of eighteen.

Two

Mosa had to spend a two years at home without looking for a job as not having an identity document was a disadvantage for her. She had to wait until her eighteenth birthday to get an identity document which would help her to start looking. Meanwhile she continued attending church and going to bible studies she even went to conferences which was paid for by the church as she was unable to pay for them herself. She would travel to places like Sunrise in Bluenburg, Bridgeville, and Freetown and a lot of other places wherever they would go whether for choir conferences, or Easter conferences which were very popular in her church. She even took it upon herself to teach Sunday school as she always had a dream of becoming a teacher. Her dream had to take a back step as she had no money for college so she had to stay home for a whole two years while her peers were going to universities and colleges. It was very difficult for her because it felt as though she has just joined all those girls with no future plans. All she had to do to keep busy was to sing in a choir, teach Sunday school and taking care of her granny and three siblings. Her grandmother was also frustrated by watching Mosa doing the same thing daily she tried to ask for financial assistance from her uncles but was unsuccessful in all her attempts. It was as if some people were meant to go to tertiary and others who are poor like Mosa were meant to only have matric and that was the highest qualification they would end up with.

The old woman ended her crusade to find funding for her granddaughter's education. She kept the hope that after she gets her identity document she will find work. All she could afford with her grant money was food and a few essentials to take Mosa's siblings through school. All that Mosa could keep herself busy was church and it really helped keep her distracted. Going to church benefited her because it kept her from the streets and from wrong company where she was going to find herself in the same path of destruction with fruits like ending up pregnant with a fatherless child like her peers in the village were. The Leuba family was really what we call poorest of the poor. They could sometimes go hungry for days and only wait for granny to go and get her grant money before they eat something. The congregation would contribute some collected cans, soup, rice and some none perishables which would help them for a while but they were not enough to hold out an old woman, three teenage girls and young boy. They always lived in hope that one of the uncles would help but it was all in vain.

Easter conference for that year was going to be held in the town called Bluenburg and as time was passing by the preparations for a trip to Sunrise were going forward. Usually the choir would practice very hard as every year the Saturday service normally became a music festival where choirs would showcase their talents. Mosa was always ready as her travel costs where covered by the church and as she was the most important member of the choir. Without her the choir was unsuccessful. The day came for the trip and they arrived on a Thursday night. The Good Friday service was separated into two services, the morning service and the afternoon service with a lunch break in between. That was the time when Mosa met this boy who was playing a keyboard for his choir, he was really good. They introduced themselves one to the other and he told her that he was from Bridgeville and she told him she was from Stoneville. His name was Richard and he was the best keyboardist at that conference. They decided to practice a song which they will perform for the next day's service. The best keyboardist and the best vocalist singing together. Richard was about five years older than Mosa.

That Saturday service choirs where performing musical items and as usual Stoneville choir was holding the first position until an announcement was made that a duo that combines Stoneville and Bridgeville was about to render an item. When Richard and Mosa took to the stage people stood and clapped because they were both favoured by everybody. Richard played his keyboard confidently and Mosa sang her lungs out. They sang so well that when they finished the crowd screamed "Ancho, Ancho" they sang and sang and sang until it was the pastor who took them off the stage.it became a conference with a difference that year, on Sunday before he can begin with his sermon he called the famous couple to sing for him. He said they should perform one last time before the conference came to an end. They performed and the conference did come to an end and as people were saying their goodbyes Richard and Mosa became very sad as their hearts had already collided and no one had told the other but their actions were very clear.

At that time there were no cell phones and only a few houses had landline phones and luckily Mosa had a neighbour who had a landline telephone. They ran there to phone in case of emergency and even receive calls. She had memorised the number so she gave it to Richard just as they were about to leave for Stoneville. He received the number and as she had told him that it was a neighbour's number, he promised to call and check if they arrived safely. He also told her that they also don't have a telephone where he lives but told her that there is a public phone at a nearby school where he was a volunteer and he promised to call. The cars pulled off and Richard and Mosa said their goodbyes, they promised to meet at the next conference which was confirmed to be held in Stoneville for the following Easter.

The trip back to Stoneville seemed to have taken too long for Mosa as she was anticipating the call from Richard. They arrived at around seven o' clock in the evening. Mosa jumped out of the car and asked her grandmother if the neighbour (Mrs Tseleka) or even her daughter (Moratiwa) came looking for her? Her granny was surprised at her behaviour that she just arrived and instead of greeting them she enquires about the neighbours. Why would Mmatseleka be looking for you? She asked. She discretely said to her in Setswana (just). Mmaleuba became curios and asked again why are you asking about our neighbour and her daughter? Did you miss them that much? Why them and not us? She only replied shortly and said "yes"

Two days went by without Mosa receiving a call from Richard. She started having many thoughts in her mind. Questions were running through her head as she was asking herself did they arrive safely. He promised to call. Maybe they had an accident on their way back home. Maybe he lost the paper the number was written on. Maybe he lied about calling. Maybe he has no money to call. Maybe, maybe and many maybes kept rolling in her mind until on the third day when Moratiwa came running to call her. The minute she saw Moratiwa she did not even give her a chance to complete a sentence when she ran to the house like a race horse. At that moment her granny was left amazed and wondering what was chasing her granddaughter. She wanted to quickly change her shirt and then they hurried to the neighbour's house and because she was in such a hurry she did not even hear the piece about Richard calling after thirty minutes. She was just in a hurry to talk to her new found friend she got so disappointed when she had to wait for another ten to twenty minutes to hear his voice. Moratiwa could not even ask who the guy was because she saw how anxious Mosa was. He called and they spoke for fifteen minutes and he promised to call again tomorrow. At that time of day Mmaseleka who was at work as domestic worker was not aware of what went on in her house? Mosa saw it fitting to inform Moratiwa about Richard, preparing her for future references. She was to call Mosa every time he called but it was supposed to be their little secret. Moratiwa agreed to be a messenger and sworn to secrecy she kept very quiet about all she knew. Richard now continued to call frequently and Mmaleuba was observing all the up and down marches to Mmatseleka's house and she pretended not to see or hear anything.

Three

The two continued talking whenever Richard had money to make a call. It was convenient for him as the public telephone was at a school where he was volunteering as an administration clerk. He was doing that work but his true love was music. He wished to become a music producer someday. He would tell Mosa about his dream of becoming a producer and Mosa would tell him about her dream of becoming a gospel singer. He would promise her that when he gets his big break he would take her as his first project. He promised to make her a star and because Mosa was in love she would laugh at his every word. Richard was this orphan who lost his parents in an awful accident when he was just five. He was raised by his uncles and their wives but they brought him up in a very good way as he was a very respectful young man with a humble soul. He had a very gentle voice which was maybe what drove Mosa crazy about him. They continued communicating until Mmaleuba started to become suspicious of Moratiwa's constant visits and every time she comes she calls her granddaughter for a phone call. Mmaleuba decided to investigate, she called in Mmatseleka and informed her of what was going on and asked her to help as the calls were received at her house. She was surprised but agreed to help investigate, she also recruited Moratiwa's younger brother who had information concerning the phone calls Mosa was receiving and how often she received them. He told them that Mosa only received calls from one Richard who was apparently calling from Bridgeville. Since they had information they decided to confront Mosa about the phone calls. The two old ladies agreed to ambush her and get her to tell them about Richard. All Mmaleuba was worried about was that Mosa was maybe pregnant and was afraid to tell them. They were right to think that way as all the young ladies in the village were going through the same thing. It was like a wrong spirit of no progress was taking over the lives of young people in that village. They had no future plans as all they did was get pregnant and have fatherless children. Mosa and Moratiwa were the only two who had a glimpse of a bright future showing in their lives. They were focused and even if they did not have money for tertiary education they were looking for jobs tirelessly and nothing like wrong friends were in their lives. Poverty was motivating them to live a positive live. With the choice they made came difficult consequences as people saw them as arrogant and proud so other young ladies in the village wanted no relationship with them. They remained friends since their first year of school and it was easy for them to remain friends because they knew and understood one another. What the old ladies was suspecting was way off the mark, their fear was really unnecessary and uncalled for as the two girls were still virgins and had made a pact to keep their virginity until they were married.

The two years wait finally came to an end, Mosa received an identity document and that became her motivation to try even harder at looking for a job. She wanted nothing less than to bring some financial relief to her granny. The day the two neighbouring old ladies decided to ambush her was wrong timing for her as she was told by somebody at church that there was a medical centre in town where there was vacancies available. She invited Moratiwa to go along with the hope that one of them would be lucky and get hired. She woke up very early and hopeful that day and as she was busy taking her bath and singing loud as usual her granny sneaked off to call Mmatseleka. They quietly came in and sat in the kitchen drinking tea as they waited for her to come out. Just as she was about to leave she was ordered to sit down, she tried to explain her haste but was cut off and told to be quiet and listen to instruction. Her grandmother even made a comment that Richard can wait as they wanted to talk to her. Mosa saw that as upcoming trouble. She asked Richard? Mmaleuba said yes! And I want to know who he is! What? Mosa exclaimed. She was shocked that her secret was out. The truth was it was out but in a wrong way as it gave the two old ladies a wrong impression. The argument between Mosa and her granny took a very long time before it got to a point. Moratiwa came to check on her but was chased away and ordered by her mother to leave without Mosa. She was worried because the job opportunity news came from her friend. They signalled by hands where Mosa told her to go and she was to meet up with her later. She left very disappointed but went ahead before Mosa to the medical Centre. After a lot of tears and words of expressing their disappointment Mosa got an idea of what they were talking about. She decided it was time to straighten things. She told them who and how she met Richard. She assured them that she was still a virgin and she also brought it to their attention that she was also disappointed that up to that far her grandmother did not trust her. She expressed herself and said "I thought you knew me better than that mme" (mme is what they called her granny, meaning mother) at that time she broke into tears as she felt insulted. She told them how she was supposed to go job hunting and for once after a long search that day was a day which had a positive promise of a job. She cried and said "now I am late and people who were supposed to go with me to where there was a prospectus job are long gone" Mmaleuba felt shameful for accusing her granddaughter, she apologised to her and told her to go. She tried to make it up to her by giving her transport money. Mosa ran out of the house crying for two reasons, one was the fact that her privacy was just invaded by two busybodies and the second reason was that she was going to lose her chance at getting a job. She got in a taxi with her eyes red, showing that she was crying. All she was hoping for was that when she gets at the medical centre, they must have space for her. As it goes; God had his plan for her life on that day. A different plan than that which she had. In the taxi there was a lady who asked Mosa why she was crying. Mosa explained to the concerned lady how she just missed her opportunity to find a job. She told her how she was just in a taxi and knew very well that no one gets a chance at that time. Tears rolled on her cheeks again and the lady gave her a tissue to wipe them away. She asked Mosa to give her one copy of her curriculum vitae and fortunately she had about four. Mosa reached in her envelope and gave the lady her CV and in return she gave her a card and told Mosa to go and drop her other CV's and if she doesn't find a job in town she must come and see her at the clinic the following day at seven o clock in the morning. Mosa agreed to the lady's arrangement and she got off the taxi and told her to stop crying. She told her just before she got off the taxi "don't worry, all will be well" she also reminded her to call the number on the card she gave her that night. Mosa agreed and the lady left. Mosa's trip continued to town and when she got there, she was already late and they hired people even Moratiwa got a job as a cleaner and there was no space for her. She was disappointed but quickly remembered the lady who said she must call her. She checked the card and kept it safe. She dropped her other CV's at the other two places and because she was in town and there were many public phones there plus she had extra money as her granny gave her money that morning she took a step and called the lady she met in the taxi. She first apologised to the lady and explained that she was phoning at that time because there were public phones at town. The lady cut her short and told her to come to the clinic the next morning and ask for Rebecca. Mosa saw that as a light at the end of her dark looking tunnel of a future. Her bad day just became better all of a sudden. When she arrived at home, she decided to warn her granny in time that she was called to the clinic just in case she decides to hold another ambush. That night Mosa rolled in her bed wondering what the next morning was holding for her.

As the saying goes " it doesn't matter how long darkness of the night lasts but the sun still have to also rise and shine" In Mosa's case the morning couldn't come sooner as she was anticipating the trip to the clinic. She kicked off her blankets at five o clock in the morning. She cleaned the other rooms as quietly as possible as she did not want to wake others. At around 05:30 am she lit the paraffin stove and filled the pot with water. Half was for her bath and the other half was for cooking soft porridge for breakfast for the whole family. She was in high spirits as if she knew that her day was going to go well. She took her well ironed church clothes and dressed very nice and clean. She combed her hair properly and took a look in a small mirror to see if she was smart enough. She wrapped herself in a clean towel to avoid smudging her clothes with a sorghum porridge as she ate her breakfast. Her granny woke up and found her eating. Mmaleuba told Mosa how anxious she was about her visit to the lady at the clinic. Mosa stood and made her tea, she also offered her breakfast but she told her she will eat later. She encouraged Mosa to go as early as possible. She was still filling very shameful about wrongly accusing her. Mosa finished eating and because her grandmother was like a mother to her she asked to pray with her. They prayed together and Mmaleuba prayed for her and gave her blessings, it became a very emotional moment as she left and her granny went in the house to wake her siblings as to prepare for school.

Four

The clinic was about fifteen minutes' drive in a taxi so Mosa left her home at twenty minutes past six, took a five minutes' walk to the tarred road and there she caught a taxi immediately so she arrived at the clinic gate at exactly 06:40 when she jumped off she did not have a watch so she asked the security guard what time it was, he gave her 06:40. The clinic was just about to be opened and people were queuing outside the yard and Mosa walked past them and followed the security guard to talk to him. The same man who gave her time a few minutes ago gave her the most frightening look as he asked her what it was. She said excuse me but I am here to see Rebecca. He rudely replied her by saying "there are many people called Rebecca there, which one was she looking for. Because Mosa did not know Rebecca's surname he told her to wait at the gate and see if she comes. Mosa was very humble and agreed to wait at the gate to see if Rebecca comes. She waited patiently as cars were coming in and outside the gate. The security guard felt remorse for her and offered her a chair because she was not a patient, she waited at the gate as it was opened for patients at 07:00. All Mosa knew about Rebecca was she met her in a taxi and how she looked. She kept dreaming about cars people were driving in and out of the clinic saying that one day she will drive that one or even that one. At exactly 07:15 a car stopped at the gate and as the widow rolled down it was Rebecca. Mosa told the guard that the lady in the car was the one she was waiting for. The guard told Rebecca about Mosa and with a welcoming smile she made a hand signal to Mosa showing her to come into the clinic. The guard told Mosa to wait for the matron as she was going to park the car. The matron? Asked Mosa in amazement. Yes, the matron said you should wait for her in the clinic, he said. Mosa went in and waited but the wait became one and a half hour long. She just sat there wondering if the matron will come or not. Rebecca came out of a room followed by many nurses who were rushing to different rooms and they seemed to be resuming their duties for the day. She came straight to Mosa and asked her to follow her. They went through the clinic reception area and as they were going in Rebecca introduced Mosa as the new filling clerk. She took her around the clinic showing her all she needed to know and every time she kept introducing her as the new filling clerk. Mosa could not believe what she was hearing, she also kept the act greeting people in a respectable manner as if she knew what was going on. To her she was just hoping that the dream better be true. She only believed it when the orientation came to an end where she was told it was the filling room, Rebecca told her that she will be working in that room and spending most of her days there. They continued to Rebecca's office where she tried to offer Mosa something to drink but because she was very nervous she refused even though she was hungry. Rebecca told Mosa that she was in the taxi the previous day because her car was taken in for a service and she said to her that now she knew that she was in a taxi to meet her. Instead of telling her the news about the job she went on and on about her car and all Mosa wanted to know was if she had a job or not. After a long speech about her car

Rebecca asked Mosa when she would start working and she was so happy she said she was ready to start on the same day but Rebecca said that she can start the following day as she was waiting for her employment contract to be delivered that day.

Rebecca just asked Mosa when she will start working but did not formerly inform her of what the job entailed and what was required of her. She quickly remembered and started talking to her telling her that she was hired as a filling clerk for the clinic, she told her that she will be working for which department and that the employment was permanent as the clinic needed a second filling clerk and that the position remained vacant until the previous day when Rebecca called the department's human resource manager and told her that she just hired a new filling clerk. She also told Mosa that she was going to work only Mondays to Fridays. She asked her to give her an identity document and a matric certificate for her to make a copies as they were required and they completed a form together. Through all this Mosa did not believe what was going on. As they were busy filling a form a man knocked on the door saying that he was delivering something for the matron. It was Mosa' employment contract and it arrived just in time. Rebecca asked the man to wait patiently as they were about to complete and she wanted the same man to deliver the contract back to head office. He waited and they completed everything and as they were busy she asked her if she had a bank account but unfortunately Mosa did not have one. Something was pushing Rebecca to help Mosa because she stopped all her work for that day and she came out of her office and she asked the delivery man to have something to eat while he waits, she told him that she and Mosa had to rush somewhere to get something. They did not tell him that they were going to the bank. Arriving at town Rebecca drove around looking for a bank with fewer people queuing. The reason was not to keep the delivery man waiting for a long time. They saw an empty bank and entered, fortunately for them Mosa was assisted immediately. At the bank Rebecca paid the R50 which was required to open a bank account. They opened an account and rushed back to the clinic, gave the delivery man all the completed documents and he drove off to take them back to the departmental head office. After all the rush they had a moment alone and Mosa got on her knees with tears of joy rolling on her cheeks as she thanked Rebecca who helped her up and wiped her tears away and said that it was nothing. She told Mosa that it felt as if something was pushing her to help her. Mosa told Rebecca the impact that job was going to have on her family, she told her about her granny and how the job was going to help relieve her financially. Rebecca told Mosa to go home and come back the following day to start working. Mosa thanked Rebecca again and because tears were coming again she stormed out to the bathroom where she fell on her knees and prayed like never before. She thanked God for all he had done that day and sang a song of worship and after that she stood up, cleaned herself and came out looking very calm. She went back into Rebecca's office to properly thank her and say her goodbyes. Just as she was about to leave she met a neighbour who had collected her medication and was about to walk home as they normally walked to and from the clinic. She asked her to join in on the journey. As they walked she started interrogating Mosa about why she was at the clinic and in the matron's office for such a long time and why did they go out and where did they rush to and come back. She made Mosa regret agreeing to walk with her because she kept asking her so many questions and all Mosa wanted to do was keep the news for her granny but the woman kept pushing and pushing until Mosa told her she found a new job. She was one of the mothers at the village who was having stress with her daughters and on top of that she was a busy body who always liked spreading news around the village. When she heard the news that Mosa found a job she was so jealous and curious but Mosa told her that she has not told her granny the news so she does not want to divulge more information. The nosey Meiki dropped the subject and they walked home quietly. She was very disappointed she did not get her gossip but she conveniently developed a thirst as they approached Mmaleuba's house. She lived a few house from the Leuba family house. The walk would take her less than five minutes but because she wanted to hear more news she just suddenly wanted water and she could only drink it at Mosa's house. Mosa allowed her to come in the yard with her as she saw her granny sitting under a tree from a distance.

When they arrived they greeted Mmaleuba and instead of drinking water and going home sister Meiki asked if Mosa could bring her a chair as she was very tired and she had long seen Mmaleuba and wanted to catch-up. Mosa brought her a chair and before she could break the news Meiki already broke the news and told granny Mmaleuba that Mosa has just found herself a job. She persuaded her to tell her granny more but Mosa told them that she was hungry and was going to make herself something to eat. She went into the kitchen and never came back until nosey Meiki got tired of waiting and left. As soon as she left Mosa came out of the house and shared the news with her granny. She told her about the amazing grace she experienced that day and she even told her about a Good Samaritan called Rebecca who she met the day before and what she did for her that day. Her granny started praising and worshiping right there and then. She asked Mosa how much her salary was but because she was too excited she did not ask how much her salary was. She quickly remembered that she had a copy of a contract and ran into the house to get it and read it to her granny, they were both shocked at the amount which was written there. Mmaleuba could not hold her tears as she was so happy that one of her granddaughters has a bright future ahead and from that time on life was going to be better. Mmaleuba asked Mosa to get Rebecca's surname as she wanted to go thank her for what she did for her granddaughter and her family.

The best news for Mosa was the office where she was going to work had a phone which meant that she was going to be able to talk to Richard without any monitoring and without anybody counting how many times and how long they talk. She was just happy that both she and her friend Moratiwa found jobs two days in a row. She waited for Moratiwa to come back home to share the news. As soon as she arrived Moratiwa and Mosa spoke and Moratiwa could not stop herself from dancing and jumping and shouting for joy. They blessed the lord for what has happened in their lives in two simultaneous days. They both said the words "this is Amazing Grace" in deed.

The night seemed very long for her as she was tossing and turning, praying and asking God what awaits her the following morning. She was so restless to a point that she woke her younger sister who shared a room with her. They spoke about how long their suffering had lasted and they kept on remembering how they suffered to a point of finding themselves washing the dishes at their uncles houses, just to be rewarded with a slice of brown bread smeared with margarine, peanut butter or strawberry jam which to them, those things were luxuries. They were reminded of how on one hungry Saturday, their younger brother went to a nearby cemetery, collected a lot of coins thrown on some tombs, how he brought them and gave them to the family without telling them were he got the money from, they remembered how they enjoyed spending it to buy vegies, maize meal and paraffin. They remembered how that night's nicely cooked dinner was spoiled by his confession of where he got the money. Even though those things were a painful memory, they also remembered how their granny taught them to always count their blessings and how when times were tough, she always smiled and told them how God would see them through. The talk continued to a point where they touched the Richard story and how Mosa was ambushed by the two old ladies but at this point in time she just laughed it off but was surprising how she forgave and forgot and that was because she loved her granny very much. At around half past four in the morning was the time when they realised how they spent the night chatting and giggling till dawn and Mosa had to start preparing for work. Realising that they decided to rather pray and wake up because they never felt sleepy anyway. Mosa was anxious and nervous about what the future was looking for her and the family. She had plans to renovate the house for her granny and her siblings. She was happy with the fact that her younger brother was no longer going to be the laughing stock of his peers because of torn clothes and shoes with holes and sometimes the jokes would go as far as the cousins laughing at her sister for not having proper underwear. They cruel children would even sometimes say how her younger brother's shoes were hungry and asking for porridge. The Leuba family had finally been rescued from shame and being ridiculed by some of the community members and even their relatives. Mosa was so sure that even if she did not want the children to notice, that night the old lady also had a very restless night too just thinking of the change her granddaughter's job will bring to their lives because truth be told, the old lady was torn apart from the inside by seeing her grandchildren suffering on a daily basis, especially on her watch and knowing very well that there was nothing she could do. The most painful part was the fact that her sons wanted nothing to do with her for as long as she was taking care of their only sister who was good at playing disappearing games whenever the children had a need or there was a requirement at school. She would promise to return with whatever was needed but it would be the last time they saw her until after a very long time when she came home with thick make-up covering her blue, black and purple bruises. She would normally come home, stay for a few days and leave without saying goodbye to anybody, not even her children. Sometimes she would even leave just like someone going to a neighbouring store to buy bread, and days would pass while they were awaiting whatever she promised to bring from the store. In other instances she would take the small boy and they will be alerted by the boy coming back alone that she was gone and never to be seen again, only after a few months will she return. Their predicament was a very unique and painful one which only the people in the situation would know how it was.

Looking from the outside you would see the four children always around the old woman and wonder where their mother or father was. The only comforting thing was Mmaleuba loved her grandchildren so much. One would have thought they were her own children. God was sustaining them though as sickness and disease was not a part of what was bothering them.

Five

The first day went very well for Mosa and she worked very hard and she was very attentive and accurate. Her co-worker even told her that she was glad to have someone release her from all the duties. They worked very hard and at the end of the day she was very tired but grateful that she has a job. The first weeks were a bit difficult as sometimes she would walk to work and back without money for transport not even some food for lunch but she persevered. Rebecca noticed that Mosa was not eating during lunch and she asked her colleague to watch and confirm her suspicions. They were true. After confirmation Rebecca called Mosa and offered her lunch the following day, she was very grateful and ate it. Rebecca knew that maybe Mosa had no food even at home that was why she did not even pack a lunch box. She remembered the day she hired her when she told her how that job was going to bring some financial relief on her granny who used to support a family of five with her pension money. Rebecca came back after lunch and told Mosa that she was going out.

She went to the shops and bought a few groceries for Mosa and her family. She came back and told Mosa to knock off at three o clock that afternoon as she was also going to a meeting in Mmanatho. She did not want their colleagues to know that she bought her things. She took her by the car and drove her to town, she then put her in a taxi and gave her money for taxi fare. She also gave her a R150 and told her that it was to help her to get to work. Because Mosa was in a taxi she just said thank you very much and Rebecca rushed off as she was running late for her meeting. Mosa just took the bags and went home in a taxi. She was just grateful that whatever was in those bags meant her family had dinner for that night.

The truth was they had no food at home and seeing Mosa from afar heavily laden with grocery bags surprised Mmaleuba because she knew that pay day was still about eleven days away. She screamed at Mosa's sister Mercy to go and help her sister. She ran and helped her bring the groceries home. Mmaleuba asked her "what is this now? Mosa replied and told her the matron gave her the bags and took her to the taxi rank. She further told her granny that Rebecca told her it was for her to pack a lunch box as she taught her that it was cheaper to carry a lunchbox at work than to buy food on a regular basis. She opened the bags with assistance from Mercy they found in the bags some toiletries, cold meats, cheese, spreads like peanut butter, fish paste and jam, tins of pilchards and baked beans, eggs, some sauces like mayonnaise, tomato sauce and mustard sauce. In those bags were some of the things which Mosa and her family were not even familiar with. They had to learn to use some things in there. Mosa also told her granny about the money Rebecca gave as taxi fair, she even made a joke and said that it was as if she knew how tired Mosa was from waking up in the morning and walking to and from the clinic. After Mmaleuba saw and heard all that she decided it was now time for her to visit the clinic.

Mosa was a very considerate young woman, she always used to put the needs of her siblings before hers. She was supposed to use the money Rebecca gave to her for transport but because they had no maize meal she sacrificed some of that money and bought a bag of maize meal for the family, which meant she had to go back to walking but she chose to walk in the mornings and catch a taxi in the afternoons. She also gave her granny money for her trip to the clinic. On that day Mosa woke up early as she was going to walk to the clinic she prepared breakfast and left some for other people in the house, packed all four lunch boxes and left for work. Her granny followed by taxi, she arrived a bit later and asked at reception to see the matron. She was told that Rebecca was not there but she chose to wait for her as she was told that Rebecca will be late that day. She waited patiently until the matron came in and was told that there was an old woman waiting to see her. She got surprised because she was not expecting anyone let alone an old lady. Mmaleuba saw Rebecca approaching and recognised her as her cousin's daughter, she exclaimed out of shock ijo! This is Emmanuel's daughter Becky. Mmaleuba and Rebecca knew each other but Mosa and Rebecca did not know that they were related. Mmaleuba did not even know that Becky was a nurse let alone a matron at their local clinic. When Rebecca saw Mmaleuba she was so happy and asked aunty is it really you? They were relatives in the instance that Mmaleuba's mother and Emmanuel's father were siblings so they were cousins which means Mmaleuba was Rebecca's aunt. They hugged and Rebecca welcomed her into her office. She was curious as to why her aunt who she had not seen in a very long time suddenly came to see her. They first caught up and spoke about family and how long it had been since they saw each other. Mmaleuba said to Rebecca that she came to thank her for helping her granddaughter with a job and for all she did for her. Your granddaughter? Rebecca asked in shock. Who is your granddaughter? Mosa, Mmaleuba replied. Ha! Mosa is your granddaughter? Wow! Whose child is she? Mmaleuba answered and said Lebo. My God; Lebo has children that are grown enough to be working? Yes Mmaleuba replied, and continued to tell Rebecca how Lebo has left her with her four children without any financial assistance or even a visit to them. Rebecca was shocked to hear what Mosa and her siblings had gone through. She was shocked to hear that she and Mosa were related. She told Mmaleuba how she met Mosa and how she always felt something pushing her to help Mosa out. She was so grateful that now she knew who Mosa was, she phoned and summoned her to the matron's office. When she got there Mmaleuba told her that Rebecca was her cousin's daughter. Mosa nearly fell off from shock. She just asked what? They embraced and after a long reconciliation party Mosa asked to be excused as she had to go back to work. Before she left Rebecca asked her to keep their relationship a secret to avoid finding themselves accused of nepotism. She agreed and left. Mmaleuba also left for home, very happy that she knew that Mosa was taken care off by family she knew that she was not to worry any more about her granddaughter at the clinic. From that time on Becky took good care of Mosa; she encouraged her in a way a mother can encourage her own daughter more especially given the fact of the absent maternal mother. She even helped her get into a correspondence cause for a diploma in office administration. She also helped her get into a driving school and passing her driving license. It was as if Rebecca was compensation after the passing of the pastor's wife. She was good influence to Mosa. On the home front Mosa became a blessing she always wanted to become to her granny and siblings. After her first salary, she made sure that she chased away hunger and poverty from the house. Her two younger sisters started to make an extra income with her assistance as she bought them sweets and chips to sell at school and the most exciting thing was the principal of the school gave them permission to do so as she knew they circumstances. Mosa saved money and renovated her granny's house, she was so hardworking until she even got her granny a borehole. Things got so easy that the Leuba family now became the envy of the village. Every time she does something at home, radio Meiki would go around the village broadcasting it to everyone. The news even reached the uncles who were rejecting them and now they would pay a surprise visit occasionally which was very odd as they detested the children so much, they were rejecting their mother for helping them. Looking at Lebo's children, it looked like they felt that their mother was only giving attention to them than she was to their children yet it was not true as Mmaleuba was only what any granny in her shoes would have done. Lebo's children had no one on earth but Mosa's cousins were born in happy homes with a mother and a father who were working good jobs and they only had the best of what life could offer. Mosa's uncles only saw them as slaves because when they were visiting they were expected to work hard before receiving a plate of food, the uncles and their wives were so cruel because Lebo's children loved visiting them as they saw what they never had in their families (a united family unit) those poor children were yearning for a mother let alone both loving parents. The evil part on the uncle's side was that they resented the children for their mother's faults. They made Mosa and her siblings to feel that they had no mother nor father. As they grew up, Mosa and Rose realised it and stopped visiting there. The young ones stopped automatically as they saw their elder sisters no longer visiting their cousins. For Mmaleuba it was easy as she had made peace with the fact that her sons were rejecting her for taking care of their only sister's children. She only called them when there was a family emergency which required their input.

While her life was heading in the right direction, Mosa was busy talking to Richard on a daily basis without anybody knowing. The elders thought the two lovers stopped talking but the truth was Mosa changed from Mmatseleka to her office number, Richard would phone every day and they would talk and talk while Mosa was at work. Even Moratiwa's brother who was mandated to spy ended without anything to report. He told the old ladies that Richard stopped calling Mosa, and she only visited Moratiwa to talk about work and how hard the corporate world was. Mosa was happy with the fact that her private life was a secret because she was a very humble child who felt shy about talking with Richard and to her it was as if she was doing something to disrespect her elders if they knew that she was in relationship even if nothing intimate was happening between them. Their long distance relationship was growing and Mosa was experiencing love and she was really happy. She continued to juggle her work, her studies, her driving lessons, her secret love life and her duties at home and at church. At her tender age she became a super woman.

Six

The Leuba family life improved a lot financially and Mosa's love life was also blossoming. They were able to enjoy and have finer things in life. Winter came and left and for the first time in many years there was no stress about warm clothes or warm food. There was enough of everything life was really comfortable. Mmaleuba and Rebecca kept contact as she was busy mentoring Mosa with her life, she would help her make good and sensible decisions. Mosa's life was really on the right track. Spring came and even the festive holidays were a breeze as they all had nice food like any other family, Mosa bought her siblings clothes and that brought joy and happiness in the family. Her family grew to respect her as she was their bread winner and to her it was all a dream come true to see poverty out of the house. As she and her best friend vowed to only lose their virginity once married, Moratiwa was the first to get married. She got married in January as they were busy preparing for the Easter conference which was confirmed at Sunrise to be held in Stoneville.

Mosa was very excited about the conference as her boyfriend who had been talking to her from last year was coming. They both anticipated the conference, they were telling each other how they can't wait till it was April to see each other. Mmatseleka was so proud of her daughter who kept herself until she was married. Moratiwa thanked her best friend Mosa for taking an oath with her to keep the boys away even when the where called names by their peers, they persevered. Months came and passed by very quickly as April's conference resumed with nice music from the voice of Mosa on a Thursday night as they were welcoming guests from far and near. All Mosa was waiting for were cars from Bridgeville and they seemed to be taking a long time to arrive. At the end of Thursday service the pastor announced that some groups were delayed and some will arrive in the middle of the night and some groups will join in on Good Friday, he did not mention the names of churches only the fact that they were delayed.

In deed some church groups arrived at midnight that Thursday and some arrived on Friday morning, some even arrived and joined in as the service continued. Mosa's heart was not really in church as she saw people from all over South Africa but not from Bridgeville. At around 12:30 the pastor was about to ascend the stage and before he could go on stage the choir from Stoneville had to welcome him with a song. They got on stage and Mosa as a lead singer, took the microphone and when she lifted her eyes to look at the front door, she saw Richard and his church members entering the church and being ushered to their seats. Her heart stopped, she felt butterflies crawling in her stomach, and her palms started sweating. She suddenly became very nervous. She quickly recollected herself and sang like she always does. She sang the second song as perfectly as the first one and as the congregation stood and clapped their hands, screaming, shouting and ululating while the pastor was ascending the stage, she ran off the stage as fast a she could, one could have thought that she was chased by someone but in fact she just wanted to get outside the church building and meet her friend Richard. The nosey Mmaleuba watched as she ran outside but because she didn't want to miss any part of the sermon, she did not follow Mosa outside. Richard also ran after her and as she was just about to take a breath there stood her handsome friend who looked straight in her eyes and said, "Hi." She replied and said "hi" back. A moment passed with eyes locked, then a warm and very long embrace followed. Mosa and Richard knew there and then that they were in love. They shared many hugs and then Mosa asked Richard why they were late. Richard told Mosa that one of the mini buses was giving them trouble and they had to wait for a replacement vehicle which took a very long time to arrive. They went inside the church after agreeing to meet during lunch break to practice a song which they were to perform for the next day. At that time they were both shy and did not know what to talk about, and where to begin because they could feel what they were feeling but none of them was ready to open up and say something so the common denominator became what they both loved which was music. To Mosa that was very strange but she did not know that Richard was also feeling weird as he was in love for the very first time. They separated and as they entered the church the clever old lady was watching and saw Richard following Mosa into the church and she said: "so this is Richard" I have finally seen him today.

The service came to a lunch break and as people were mingling Mmaleuba met with the pastor's wife from Bridgeville. It was not the first time they met, they knew each other from women conferences where they used to sit and talk. Mmaleuba did not know that Mmamoruti and Richard were related. They spoke for a while and got to the point where Mmaleuba enquired about Richard from Mmmamoruti who asked why Mmaleuba wanted to know about his nephew. She told her how after the previous year's Easter conference Richard and Mosa were communicating on a daily basis and she kept wondering what happened in Sunrise because Richard was the one phoning their neighbour's house daily and they would talk for a very long time. Mmamoruti told Mmaleuba that Richard was her late brother's son. She explained that he lives a few streets from her house and she confirmed that he was a good and well behaved boy. She further told her about the terrible death of both his parents twenty two years ago in an accident, how he was left only with his older sister who was currently married but still takes care of him. Mmamoruti told Mmaleuba that he had enough money but still volunteers at a local primary school and he does not rely on his inheritance instead he loves music so much he wanted to go to Bluenburg to pursue a music production career. At that time Mosa and Richard approached them to introduce one another to their parents as they shared their stories as well. They left nothing they really shared all their life stories and all that was left was for them to meet each other's guardian. They were actually surprised by the fact that their guardians knew each other. The two lovers made it a very short introduction as they wanted to spend more time together before the second service resumed. After a short meet and greet Mosa and Richard left to give their mothers some gossip time and in deed they started talking again. Mmamoruti told Mmaleuba how she observed Mosa through the conferences and she saw her to be a well behaved child. Mmaleuba told her the story of Mosa's life and completed by telling her that grace has come to their house by the same girl who has now become a bread winner for their family. The two ladies spoke and their conversation ended with an agreement to marry Richard and Mosa before they fell into temptation. Mmamoruti promised Mmaleuba to arrange everything. She promised to talk to her husband who was supposed to convince Richard to make a decision and they were to take it from there. The conference came to an end with the performance of the duet as usual who sang their best and who were loved by everybody in church. After their last song people said their goodbyes and the two promised to talk on the phone and also promised to see each other at the next conference. They were not aware of what was planned for them.

Mmamoruti had a landline number and her and Mmaleuba exchanged numbers as Mosa had improved their life to a point that she even installed a landline phone at their home. While Mosa and Richard made their arrangement to talk on a regular basis the two ladies completed their arrangement also. Everybody went home and all Mmaleuba kept praying for was what she and Mmamoruti agreed to do. She had accepted that Mosa was to get married someday as her best friend was already married and had moved to Bluemountein. Mosa showed signs that she was lonely because her one and only best friend had left her and she really missed their time together, how they used to gossip and even shared advises. Mmaleuba thought that maybe the excitement of planning her own wedding will bring back the smile on her face.

One day Mosa came back from work and found Mmaleuba on the phone from Bridgeville and she overheard how the two ladies were agreeing that on the same night Mmamoruti planned to talk to her husband about Richard marrying Mosa. She became furious that people were meddling in her life and no one consulted her. The following morning she phoned the school very early to warn Richard, but little did she know that all she told him was falling exactly into what Richard had intended. Mosa did not realise that Richard was trying to propose to her but did not have the guards to tell her so she actually alerted him not knowing that it was exactly what he wanted the elders were on the right track as he was going to agree with what the elders proposed. He was very excited about the news. The minute the Pastor came to him he could not say yes fast enough. Mmamoruti called Mmaleuba with the great news and at that time the poor woman thought it was time to break the news to her granddaughter who unfortunately for Mmaleuba, already knew and was not ready to commit to an arranged marriage. She was not as excited as everyone about the news. Mmaleuba was surprised at Mosa's reaction as she thought that she would be excited but her reaction was fury because the elders where meddling in their affairs and it made her very uncomfortable. Mmaleuba seeing that she was not getting through her granddaughter, tried to explain that they were arranging the marriage as a preventative measure. Mosa shouted with a loud voice of anger asking: prevention from what? What exactly? Mmaleuba replied "fornication" {which is a sin committed when a man and a woman have sex before they are married}. She further explained to her that they might fall into temptation and succumb to the lust of the flesh. Mosa angrily asked her grandmother how she and Richard would succumb to the lust of the flesh when they were in a long distance relationship, a very, very new relationship for that matter. Mmaleuba continued to annoy Mosa further by telling her how she too was a young woman and how she knew how youth behaved. Mosa got furious that her granny did not trust her to make her own decisions about her own future and stormed out of the house angry.

She ran and as she was running on her own she made the decision to wait for Richard to propose but if he didn't she was never going to agree to an arranged marriage. She knew and understood that all the elders were thinking about was the fact that the children might disgrace them, they had seen a lot of disappointment in the church were parents would be proud that their children are getting married, but soon became disappointed as they found out that the young woman was already pregnant sometimes even with another man's child not even her suitor. Mmaleuba was trying to prevent that but her mistrust was truly unfounded as Mosa and Richard never even had their first kiss. Mosa was the most determined young lady she did not make rush decisions, she was stable and always had her head thinking straight. When she started something, she would not stop until she completed it. She had made a pact with a friend to keep her virginity and that was what she decided to do with her life. She was just introduced to the strange feelings of loving someone, as she was trying to learn and adjust to the strange feeling of being in love with someone. Then suddenly she was expected to marry him that soon. To Mosa all that was not fair. She went back home and found her granny waiting for her and to get her off her back she told her that she needed a few days to think about the matter knowing very well she wanted to talk to Richard about it first. The next morning Richard called Mosa and proposed formally and even told her the news that the school had just made his administration position permanent. Mosa would not even hear the news she was disappointed that Richard did exactly what in some weird way she expected him to do. She saw that she was at crossroads and consulted Rebecca on the matter. What surprised her was the fact that Rebecca was happy for her but she gave her advice on the matter at hand. She advised Mosa to follow her own heart, she even told her that there is nothing wrong in prolonging the wedding plans to allow her time to get to know Richard better. Rebecca gave her the advice she needed after that she plugged up the courage, called Richard and asked him to give her time to think about his proposal. She told him how a lot had to be considered before taking such drastic steps in life. He agreed to give her time to think but was very disappointed and kept wondering how somebody had to think about a marriage proposal. He thought Mosa would be excited but it showed that she was one of a kind, unlike other young women she did not jump for joy at his proposal. When a young woman is in love and had just been proposed to she became happy and her face is always glowing but it was a different story, she was stressed about her siblings and her granny as to who was going to fend for them when she got married. To her it was depressing to even hear the word marriage. She was worried that she did not even know how to take care of a husband. All she knew was that she just fell in love with Richard and now she had to face two families who were forcing her to make a decision about marriage. She was stuck between her family welfare and her unpredictable happiness. For her it was all too soon and the fact that Richard was infatuated enough to agree to marry her that soon became pressure on her. All she did was pray for God to give her the wisdom to face that challenge and come out of it no matter what happened.

Seven

Mosa prolonged things by ignoring Richard's phone calls and whenever he forced to speak to her she said it was because she was thinking about it. Two months passed away and by that time Mosa was still thinking about the matter. Mmaleuba decided to confront her, and she answered by telling her granny that she was still thinking about it, and people had to be understanding as she had a lot to consider. The old lady asked her what she was considering but she only told her it was personal and private. Richard saw that Mosa was reluctant to marry him and it seemed like the elders were hitting a brick wall when it came to that matter. He decided to take matters into his own hands. He asked permission from the pastor to buy Mosa an engagement ring. The pastor was against it as an engagement ring was supposed to be presented after the dowry was paid. Richard convinced his elders that times have changed and people give out engagement rings all the times even before the dowry had been paid. He told them that her answer to the proposal would be the final one, if she said yes to the engagement ring it would mean the wedding preparations will go on, but if she said no to the ring it meant that he would give up pursuing her. They ended up agreeing with him to try his plan out. They agreed because they saw how passionate about the matter he was. It meant he was really in love with Mosa.

He went and bought a beautiful engagement ring. He made an arrangement to stay with a friend from church while he visited Stoneville for a weekend. The Bogosi family agreed to keep out of their business and let the children decide on their own what they wanted for their lives. Mmamoruti called Mmaleuba and informed her about Richard's decision to visit Stoneville to try and speak to Mosa on his own. Mmaleuba told Mmamoruti about her fears that if the children were to spend a lot of time together; they might fall into temptation, and she assured her that Richard promised to only talk to Mosa. She further told her that he arranged to stay with his friend from church so he won't trouble them. Friday afternoon Richard packed and left for Stoneville. He arrived at a friend's house that night and made an arrangement to meet Mosa on Saturday morning. Mosa agreed to meet him at ten in the morning as Saturday was her laundry day, so she had to wake up in the morning, do her chores, after everything was done and only when the laundry was hanged she would have time to see him. He walked to her house and collected her. They went on a tour, she showed him around Stoneville as they were talking. For the first time in her life Mosa felt close and very comfortable with Richard. They spoke, made jokes, laughed and even chased one another alongside the banks of the dam. Richard told Mosa how beautiful and peaceful that place was. They held hands just before he bowed down on his knees, took a ring out of his pocket and proposed to her. She became speechless for a while and politely asked him to stand up from his knees. He was shaking, thinking that she just rejected him. He stood up and tried to beg her but she stopped him. She asked him if they could sit on the grass. They sat down and Mosa started to explain to Richard why she was reluctant to marry him. She said to him: it is not like I don't want to marry you; I have a lot to consider, like I am a bread winner at home. He tried to intercept but she stopped him by putting her finger on his mouth and saying, shhhh! I am not finished. Richard; yes! You might be an orphan; but you told me you have an inheritance you can use. For me I inherited Rose, Mercy, Joshua and my granny, I have to take care of them and I can't do that when I am married and have my own family responsibilities. I am busy with my diploma and I want to graduate before I get married, plus Rose is in standard nine and I at least have to help pay her school fees until she completes her matric. I can't accept your marriage proposal because I come with a lot of baggage and I am not sure if marriage should add to my stress right now. Richard held her hand and said to her: I understand all that but does it mean that you will not marry me? For real? Because I love you and I want no one else but you. I am willing to wait until you graduate and get your diploma, I am even willing to pay for you and your sister Rose's education. She rejected his offer to use his inheritance money to pay for her and Rose's education. They continued talking until Richard came up with an idea of how all that could work out. Richard proposed a prolonged courtship, which would mean by the time they got married all will be sorted on Mosa's part. She agreed to his plan and told him to propose again which he did and because all was sorted out between the two she gladly agreed. He gave her the ring and because she also believed in wearing a ring once the dowry was paid she put it on her necklace and promised to keep it safe until the day of their traditional wedding. They also agreed on some suitable dates to go present each to their elders. For the first time ever since they met they sealed their agreement and their engagement with a kiss. That was their first confirmation of their love and because they were alone they enjoyed their privacy, but kept in their minds to avoid temptation.

The day seemed to have been too short for the lovers because it was a winter day and at that time of the year days just disappeared plus Richard had to catch a taxi back to Bridgeville, they said their goodbyes and Richard went back home victorious. He arrived home and told the elders what he and his fiancé had agreed on. He gave the elders the green light to start preparing for a journey to Stoneville. Mosa also got home that Saturday night after seeing Richard off at a taxi rank. She humbly asked her granny for an audience as she had news. Mmaleuba was so nervous as if she was the one about to be disappointed. Mosa told her granny she agreed to marry Richard but there were conditions they agreed upon. Mmaleuba asked: conditions? What conditions? She said to her that they agreed to have a long courtship. She continued to tell her that Richard agreed to wait for her to complete her diploma and for Rose to complete her matric while Mosa was going to try and get her the voluntary position at the clinic to make sure that when Mosa resigns Rose has the experience to do her job; that way Mosa was to get married and not worry about the family going back to the poor state they were in before. She told her granny about the ring and presented the dates she and Richard agreed upon. Richard was also doing the same presentation in Bridgeville. That month was July and she suggested to Mmaleuba that the Bogosi family can come visit in September and they were to have their traditional wedding in December. The two lovers also agreed that after the traditional wedding, they were ready to marry a year from there. Mosa told her granny that by that time she would have completed her diploma and Rose would have completed her matric and on top of that Mosa told her granny that she also wanted to make sure she saved enough money for her wedding and to leave the family with a lump sum which will assist the family for a while. The old lady was so happy that the two reached an agreement and promised her granddaughter to follow and adhere to all their conditions. It was after all the two who were getting married so they had to say what goes where and when it goes. The Bogosi family also agreed to abide by the couple's rules of engagement. They called the next morning and arranged an introduction ceremony which was held on the twenty second of September. Mosa and her family had to get started with the preparations as both the introduction and traditional ceremonies were to be held at their home.

Mmaleuba knew that the difficult part was to inform family and most importantly her daughter, Lebo {Mosa's biological mother}. She always avoided family meeting as they always ended in drama. That was supposed to be the most joyous time to her but once she started thinking about her dysfunctional family, her mood turned sour. She first called Mosa's siblings and informed them. Before they could hear all the facts naughty Mercy spoke out of turn and asked; who will feed them when their sister and only breadwinner was getting married. She asked how they were going to survive poverty again. She was seriously concerned and her eyes were even tearing up. Mmaleuba stopped her from talking and instructed her to remain quiet until she was done talking. Mercy was a very stubborn child whatever she did, she did! And no one could stop her. No one could tell her what to do or even say. She had a will of her own and the family had accepted her the way she was, they even nicknamed her "hot head". After Mmaleuba stopped her from talking she stormed out of the room angrily. They continued their conversation with granny telling them everything from the plans their sister had made of prolonging her engagement for their sakes and how she plans to try and help Rose to get a job before she gets married. Rose became very grateful at her sister for sacrificing a lot and prolonging her marriage and happiness just for the family, she felt very pitiful that at that time she had to put her life on hold because of them but Mosa told Rose how blood is thicker than water, and how it would be useless to jump into marriage where she would not enjoy because her heart would always be wondering what her family was eating or if they were warm for winter. It became a very emotional day for the Leuba family but it was all in a joyful manner. They all prayed and went to bed. That night Mosa could not sleep as she had so many thoughts of how many changes were happening and were still going to happen in her life and all in less than five years.

That Sunday morning Mmaleuba told Mosa that she had to inform the pastor about the matter at hand. The pastor welcomed the news and gave his blessings to the family, he also offered to have a helping hand in Mosa's wedding arrangement as Mosa was a vital member of the church. They prayed for the matter and the pastor arranged for Mosa to start attending marriage counselling, he further promised to contact the Bridgeville pastor to tell them to start Richard on marriage counselling also. The news of the wedding took over the Leuba family, they had many arrangements to do before the introduction ceremony. That afternoon after church Mmaleuba called a family meeting to delegate the four children as to who will do what for the whole family meeting which was to be held the following Saturday. Mmaleuba had three sons and one daughter. They were all married and all had their own homes where they lived with their wives and children. Only Lebo stayed with her husband while her children stayed with Mmaleuba. Lebo was a very touchy subject as her mother did not want her to be a part of the wedding but Mosa thought it to be a great idea, just to show her how she missed out on her children growing up to a point where one of them was getting married. The children were all delegated to go to their uncles' houses to spread the invitation to a family meeting which was to be held the following Saturday. Mercy was given two tasks, to fist walk to her mother's house and summon her home on Wednesday to avoid her hearing the news on the streets or at the family meeting when the old lady would be announcing to everyone. There after she was to go to her other uncle who lived close by her mother's house. Rose was given a task to take the invitation by taxi as the other uncle lived a bit far, you could only reach his house by taxi. Joshua was given a simple task to walk to the uncle who lived not too far from Mmaleuba's house, he also lived about thirty minutes' walk away but in a different direction. They all went to bed that night with everyone knowing his or her responsibility for the next day. The next morning was very cold and Mosa woke up and prepared herself for work, she left her granny to deal with her other siblings who did not want to wake up as they complained about the cold. Mercy complained the most. As the sun was rising and it was warming up they all took the road to deliver the messages. They were all successful and the meeting between mother and daughter went awkwardly as Mercy was very uncomfortable at her mother's house. She was offered some food and drinks but rejected everything. She only sat down to give to her mother the message and then quickly asked for a way as she was sent to her uncle's house. Her mother received a message and promised to show up on Wednesday. Mercy said her goodbyes and proceeded with her journey. At the end of Monday the news had spread to all family members about a meeting but they all knew nothing about the wedding. Mmaleuba had instructed the children not to give away any information as the news were to be broken to Mosa's mother first on Wednesday and the uncles were to be told on Saturday. The children were respectful to their granny and mentioned not even a hint to anybody, even naughty Mercy kept the secret to everyone's surprise. Lebo came home that Wednesday in the morning as she was summoned. Mosa had already left for work and because of the winter holidays her sisters and brother were still in bed when their mother arrived. Their grandmother was awake and as usual; she was drinking her tea. Mosa's mother was told the news and she responded coldly as expected because she did not have any joyous bone in her body as her husband had beat it out of her; or maybe it was the shame that made her hide her true feelings about her firstborn getting married. She spent the whole day at Mmaleuba's and during that day her children could not even say a word to her, they did not even know how to address her as Mosa called her Aunty, the ten year old Joshua could not even stay in the same room with her. He avoided facing her, because they had no maternal feeling or any connection, he knew Mmapaledi as his mother and even called her mama. Lebo somehow showed remorse through the day as her children were treating her like plague. That afternoon Mosa arrived from work and found her mother in the kitchen drinking tea. It was her last cup before she could leave for her house. There was a silent moment between them understandably because she would spend a long time without visiting even though she lived about forty five minutes away. It took a while before she could say congratulations to Mosa and Mosa responded coldly saying: "thank you" and then the silence followed again. Finally Mmaleuba came in and informed Mosa that the family meeting on Saturday was confirmed and she had to take care of the food for her uncles and their wives. Mosa's mother tried to show some effort and interest in her daughter's affairs by coming every morning that Thursday and Friday to help with arrangement for the big family meeting.

The meeting went well by the grace of God they all agreed to give Mosa and Richard their way. The uncles agreed to the dates, both for the introduction ceremony and for the traditional wedding. Mmaleuba kept a few of Mosa's personal reasons for her demands. Fortunately for her they agreed to abide by her request. The only true but unpleasant part of the meeting was the fact that Lebo was excluded from all the wedding arrangements as they said it was because of her abusive husband; she was found to be unreliable. It was painful to Mosa but there was nothing she could do about it. The only positive thing about all that was the fact that she was going to have an excuse to see and spend time with her children. Even if she pretended to be strong but the fact that she was kept away from her children was killing her. The problem was she did not want to accept the fact that her husband was abusing her, she was too shy to admit that her husband prohibiting her from seeing the children was wrong. In the meantime her children were growing and hating her every day of their lives for neglecting them by the day. She did not even know how to address her son because his story was the most painful as she left him when he was only two weeks old and returned when he was six years old, only to leave again and became a stranger yet living in the same village as them. The pain was slowly showing as she would now and then wipe a tear from her cheek when nobody was watching. Every time she spoke to her children they would be very cold, rejecting and defensive towards her. It was as if they were afraid to get close to her, knowing that she was going to be there only for a short while and fly out of their lives like she always did. It was the children's way of defence, or even their way of protection against the pain they were to feel after their mother deserted them yet again. It was as though they spoke before but they never even discussed how they were all going to react towards their mother, it happened automatically because their feelings were mutual. Even though it was difficult for Lebo, she had to grin and bear with consequences of her actions, choosing men over her children and mother. Their granny was the most brave as she had to go through the pain of watching her own flesh and blood do what she did again and again. She had to watch and raise each and every fatherless child from Lebo with the hope that one day she was going to one day grow up to become a decent woman she had brought her up to be. During the time of the planning of Mosa's marriage, the old lady was just praying and hoping that Lebo should apologise for all her mistakes and rectify them by building a relationship with her children. The fact was she knew that she was hoping for a very, very hopeless situation. All she kept praying for was staying power for Mosa in her marriage; looking at her mother's track record with men and counting how many suiters came knocking at her door, asking for Lebo's hand in marriage but just after a dowry was paid, something would go wrong and her promiscuous daughter would come home with her face covered in blue and black bruises. Soon after she was healed, she would disappear like water on dry ground; which meant she met another man and has moved on from the previous one. The only collateral damage caused was that all her children were born out of all those useless relationships and because their mother had some unresolved issues with all those men, she ended throwing herself in the hands of a woman beater who not only abused her physically, financially and emotionally. He kept her locked up away from her family and friends which was why he was not even part of Mosa's wedding preparations. None of Lebo's brother wanted anything of his nor his presence where the family was concerned and looking at his behaviour the whole family was treating her like a stranger and not Lebo's husband. Mmaleuba kept it together for the sake of all the family and she was the strongest in the whole family. All this happened while the preparations were going forward.

The set date arrived for the introduction ceremony and everything went well. The two families agreed to have a traditional ceremony on the fourteenth of December and they also agreed that all will be discussed by phone if something was to occur and hinder the plans. The traditional wedding was planned in a way that it was to allow Mosa to turn twenty five in November. At the introduction ceremony the two families agreed that Richard would visit Stoneville to attend couple's counselling and they arranged someone from each family to accompany them. That was to happen every time they met until their white wedding happened. This was to distract them and prevent them from falling in to temptation which may lead to them committing a sin called fornication. In the Christian believe it was supposed to be like that because even if the dowry had been paid Richard and Mosa were not allowed to sleep together until they were blessed at their white wedding. All this they knew and understood very well. They could steal a kiss here and there but Mosa was supposed to remain a virgin until her wedding night. Their traditional ceremony also went well and the full dowry was paid but Mosa remained behind and was not taken to her in-laws as per agreement that she was to be married in a white wedding first. Richard and his family returned home after the ceremony and life went as if nothing happened for a whole year. He would visit Stoneville for the two to attend counselling with their shepherds and spent a little time with her. Easter conference came and they enjoyed it. The preparations were also going very well and to everyone's surprise Lebo showed commitment to helping her daughter through all her wedding preparations. She stood up to her husband for the first time in her life, and told him that her daughter needs her and she was there not only for Mosa; but she was there for all her children and since her often presence at her home, they were warming up to her. As per promise in June that year Mosa got Rose a voluntary position at the clinic. She jumped right on it but after she wrote her final matric examinations, when she was expected to apply for a filling clerk position; she found her own permanent position somewhere else. That pleased Mosa to see that that not only did her sister show confidence; but her family was taken care off financially. She resigned at the end of November to give herself a chance to finalise wedding arrangements as the day was very close. At that time she graduated and got her office administration diploma but she did not celebrate because all the money was put into the wedding of her dreams plus she wanted to fulfil her promise to leave the family a lump sum of money to keep them afloat for a while.

The fifteenth of December, which was the long awaited morning and the biggest day of Mosa and her lover; Richard to become husband and wife arrived. She woke up and because there were people from everywhere working, cooking, singing and ululating it just hit her:" I am getting married", she repeated it again with tears from her eyes: "I am getting married". While she was busy wallowing in her emotions her matron of honour and best friend Moratiwa came in and reminded her that on her wedding day; Mosa encouraged her to be strong and now Moratiwa also encouraged her to be strong and get through the day. Besides Moratiwa's wedding; there were no wedding ceremonies or any celebrations of that sort in that village until the day of Mosa's wedding so the whole village stood on its feet to watch how the family which was known to be the poorest in the village host all their guest in celebration. The bride prepared and with her mother by her side, she left her home for the church in style. That was Mosa' dream of the biggest wedding their village had ever seen becoming true that day. With her family as her entourage; her one and most special friend and her siblings went to church in cars hooting and listening to the whole village singing and ululating behind them. It really was a special day and both Mmaleuba and Lebo shed a tear of joy now and then. All the way to church, Mosa kept asking Moratiwa to pinch her as she was in a very strange dream and expecting to wake up from it any minute. Even when they reached the church grounds and saw people standing outside the church, in their beautiful garments; to her it was like she was at somebody's wedding. She was in another world of disbelieve and all was to be verified the moment she saw Richard in her dream world jumping off the decorated vehicle. Looking at him; her heart skipped a bit faster as her best friend whispered to her ear, "your hubby to be is here". She huffed and puffed as if she was going to faint until she felt the warm hand from her biological mother which touched hers as she said to her "worry not child, God is with you so All is well". For the first time in her life Mosa felt the maternal bond between them and it was just at the right moment; as if Lebo knew her duty to calm Mosa and comfort her mother through it all. Mosa felt very confident after her mother told her the inspiring words, she now looked forward to her vow exchange with the love of her heart. The people entered the beautifully decorated church, the groom waiting at alter with his entourage, his uncle and the pastor {who was also one of his uncles} by his side. Every one entered except a blushing bride and her brother. She chose to be walked down the aisle by her one and only brother as they knew nothing about their biological father, they tried to persuade Mmaleuba and Lebo to tell them about him but they were denied the information for years. She opted to be given away by her brother. As she walked down the idle, her hands dripped with sweat, her heart pumped like never before and it was as if her steps would just move back and not forward. To her mind questions started to overflow and flood her little head. She realised that there was no turning back just as she steadfastly held on her brother's hand who noticed how scared she was, and with a soft kiss to the cheek; he whispered into her ear. "I am hear for you and I love you very much". He walked her until he presented him to Richard's hand with one of her uncles approaching as he instructed Richard to take good care of Mosa or else. Richard was also not having it easy. He was also fighting his own butterflies and trying very hard to keep the ears of joy away. On the third row seated the three most important ladies in Mosa's life who were also wiping away a tear or two from their cheeks. Mmaleuba, Lebo the neighbour (Mmatseleka) and the wife to the elder uncle who were nicely dressed but were also sharing a sombre moment as they witnessed their beautiful daughter's walk to wife and motherhood. For the first time in a very long time Lebo and Mmaleuba held each other's hand in support. The congregation stood in honour of the bride until the Man of God showed them by a hand signal to be seated. As according to the couple's request the pastor blessed and announced that they were married in a very short matrimonial Ceremony. The couple and the families had agreed to have a short matrimonial ceremony and then all the speeches were to be done at the reception. The celebrations began with the couple leaving the church, dancing to the music. The cars spinning on the dusty village streets but with crowds enjoying every moment in anticipation to see the newly married couple jump of their decorated car. The bride's mates and grooms men hanging out of car windows, waving white handkerchiefs. The festivities continued as they proceeded into the reception tent which was beautifully decorated and it got filled with people who started eating like they were told that food was going out of production in less than twenty four hours from that moment. Their stomachs and for some; handbags even clothing pockets nearly burst full of food and canned drinks. Old people held crystal glasses for the first time in their lives. For some, it was the first time they held a fork and knife ever since they were born. The Leuba family home had just thrown their grandchild her dream wedding and everybody there saw it. Mosa was the happiest of them all. Her two sisters and brother were also glad that their mother shared the special moment with them. She and Mosa got very close during that time and her siblings also forgave and got close to their mother. The wedding continued and ended on a sour note when the Bogosi family had to take their daughter in law to Bridgeville. She cried and said goodbye to her family. Her uncles and aunts accompanied her but she was still crying until they reached Bridgeville. Most of the family and close friends followed the next day to attend her welcoming ceremony which went very well. There was also plenty of everything, food and drinks and everybody was happy. The Bogosi family threw her the biggest ever welcoming ceremony and invited lots of people, it was the same as the previous day when the villagers came to see an orphan boy who was getting married to the most beautiful bride from Stoneville. When time came for the Leuba family and friends to leave Bridgeville Mosa's mood turned sour again as she now realised that she will be left in a strange house with her new family to start her life there. She cried a lot but her husband comforted her with a surprise. He gave her a honeymoon voucher for them to go and spend Christmas in Mozanice and suddenly her sour mood changed and became happy. They left the following morning for their honeymoon and had a great time. They got back from their honeymoon on the thirtieth of December and enjoyed the last of the festive season with Mosa's new found family. She welcomed the New Year as Mrs Bogosi and two weeks after the New Year she was permitted to visit her family. They went there just before Richard could go back to work. He had in the previous year applied for a job at a music studio in Bluenburg and was waiting for the results. They visited Stoneville and Mosa's family was very happy to welcome them and spend time with them.

Richard had spoiled his new wife with a new cell phone and he also had one for himself. They got back from Stoneville and Richard found a message back home that the record studio called and set an interview appointment for him. He was so excited; he went with his wife for a second one week honeymoon in Bluenburg where he was called for an interview. They booked and stayed in a guest house near the music studios where he went for an interview and they stayed a few days after with the hope that Richard will get the results but it did not happen. They went back to Bridgeville as Richard went back to his work at school as an administrative assistant leaving his wife at home with the promise that Mosa will look for a job and also start working. Richard worked for two months before he received a phone call from the music studios in Bluenburg. He came back from work one day and shared the good news that he had been offered a position in Bluenburg and they were to leave very soon. The job came with a fully furnished flat and a car so for the newlyweds; the job was a real blessing. They moved immediately after Richard had put his resignation forward at the school. They moved into their new flat and Richard started his new job happily; still with the promise to allow his wife to look for work as soon as they were completely settled. He also reminded her of his promise to make her a gospel music star as soon as he started producing. Mosa kept hope that one day her husband shall let her look for a job or even let her help build a singing career. Richard was only concentrating on his career and kept telling his wife that when things are settled she will start looking for work.

Eight

They moved to Bluenburg in March and they stayed there for three months and just when Mosa thought that things had settled, she found out that they were expecting their first child. Three months pregnant and after six months she gave birth to their first born son and named him Thatoyaone which meant God's will. They called him Thato for short. That was in the first month of the year. All that changed Mosa's life plan as she now had to stay home and care for their child. She suddenly became a house wife and continued to take care of their son who after two years and three months they discovered that he was going to have a sibling. Her career dreams were fading as she now had to take care of the toddler and carefully go through her second pregnancy. While that was going on Richard's career grew and he was even busy with negotiations to start a partnership in Richetown. Things sped up and Richard's business deal came through where he got the chance to head up the new music company in Richtown. He took a piece out of his inheritance and went into partnership where they began their own record label. That was his dream come true. With that came hope for Mosa who remembered her husband's promise to make her a music star. He promised to take Mosa on as his first project as soon as he made it in the music industry as a producer but Richard was busy with his own dreams he did not even care about his previous promise to his wife. To him it was all about his ambitions, nothing and no one mattered. The time to move to Johannesburg arrived and at that time poor Mosa was six months pregnant with their second child and she also had Thato as a toddler; so the move was very stressful for her. They had to ask both her sisters, Richard's sister and her husband to help with the move. Richard bought them a house in a suburb called Sundown and as the family members were fussing over Mosa; he became jealous because nobody recognised and congratulated him on his achievements. They had their first big fight while his and her family members were still visiting them. Their siblings had to leave on a very sad note because Richard felt jealous that they were supporting and pampering his pregnant wife. It was as if he wanted people to sing praises because he had made it in life and even managed to buy a very big mansion for him and his family but a simple congratulations was not enough. He noticed how they were loving and faffing around his wife and he felt left out. He just busted started to hurl insults at his wife for no reason. Mosa was left shocked and disappointed at his behaviour that he portrayed in front of their guests. She just kept wondering what went wrong because all was well until he suddenly screamed and it was even unusual because he had never had any of those episodes before. Days passed before he apologised for an unpleasant situation he caused and they moved on. A few weeks after that Mosa gave birth to the most beautiful girl and called her Joy. Richard continued to get swallowed by the big city life and the music industry to a point that he started to neglect his duties as a father and a husband. Mosa was left with no choice but to become a house wife; raise two children and just forget about her future plan or even dreams she had. The only help Richard brought home was he hired a house help saying that was his way of releasing his wife of house chores, so Mosa can pay her full attention to the children. He worked very hard, spent most of his days and seldom nights in studio or at business meetings. Mosa was observing all that and she saw how her husband was slowly slipping away from their home.

Richard was good at what he does. He produced good music to a point that after a while he bought out his business partner and he was left the sole owner as his partner left the country and went to pursue other avenues abroad. He never changed the name of the record label because RB records was the original name formed by Richard and his partner's first initials but he decided to keep the name in a sense that it was also a first alphabet from his surname. So because he had built a name and he had a good reputation, musicians were queuing at his door looking for recording deals. He became very big and famous but what was surprising was he was alone in all of that as if he had no family. Mosa was not even featuring in any of his events not even a mention of a wife or children. It was like they don't exist in his life. To every launch he would either take a friend or go on his own. Mosa confronted him and he lied to her and said he was protecting them from the media and did not want his personal life splashed all over the papers which was surprising because his face was on every social page of every weekend paper. Mosa brought up the two children with the help of her domestic worker Lorraine and she thanked God for her because she was very supportive. It was like she was compensation for her sisters who were burned by her husband from visiting Mosa. She respected and helped Mosa and she even became Mosa's confidant. She would share with her all that was wrong in her life and all her worries and fears. She always advised and prayed with Mosa and the children. Richard started with his mischievous ways, he would travel to London for weeks and not come home. He avoided been intimate with his wife all seemed to be falling apart. When Mosa told his family he became violent and he prohibited her from visiting his home and he stopped her from talking to family members. She was coached whenever they went to family gatherings; to play a role as a happily married woman. She did as she was told and her reward became a one night of passion where she realised after a few months that she was pregnant with their third child. That brought more stress on her to a point that she developed high blood pressure.

His dirty laundry was splashed across the papers week after week and his explanation would be "that woman is my colleague", I work with her and in the meantime pregnant Mosa carried the responsibility of explaining to other family members and relatives that she was busy with children so Richard had to take their friend to the function. She lied to everyone and the only person who knew the real truth was Lorraine and kept it a secret as she was a loyal friend even though it was a very painful secret to keep. Mosa was busy dying a slow death emotionally just like her love to sing praise and worship was killed by her husband. He stopped attending church with them because going to church meant playing family and he was not that keen on going to church holding hands with his wife or be seen playing the father role to his children. He changed from that sweet man who loved Mosa and turned into a monster who hurled insults at his wife and children any chance he got. At first he would abuse her physically and bring home presents and as time went on he would beat her to the pulp, leave and stay away for days, not even phoning to check if she was fine. She kept it all between her and their house maid. Loraine advised her to lay charges against him but he could swindle himself out of anything by either smooth-talking or even bribing his way out of any mess. One day he fought with a seven month pregnant Mosa to a point that Mosa went into premature labour, he got scared and rushed her to the hospital where she gave birth to a very small premature baby. He apologised and for a few weeks he supported his wife and their baby but a call came in and he left for days without even a phone call to check if the mother and her child were fine. When he came back he had excuses but Mosa was so familiar with every excuse he made; she was actually tired of hearing them. He hang with bad company and Mosa grew to the suspicion that he was experimenting with drugs because one day Mosa went out and found a cd cover on the table with a residue of white powder on it. She called the maid and showed it to her asking who was using the cd and Lorraine answered with:" it was Mr Richard". Mosa confronted him and she got all lies and as usual he stormed out of the house very furious. The third child grew under those difficult conditions with other children going to school at that time. On the home front, the situation was going from bad to worst. The children grew up watching their mother been insulted, called names and beaten so much they grew to hate their father. The young boy would ask his mother why they were still staying there. She would respond by telling him that their father loves them very much and he was just stressed about work but she promised him that all was going to be well in due time. The little boy because he was older taught his two little sisters the trick of avoiding hearing their dad curse their mom. He taught them to put their hands over their ears and cover their ears so tight, they won't hear anything.

One day a newspaper published a picture of Richard in a very unpleasant and compromising position. At that time Mosa could not avoid it as she woke up to calls flooding in from family and church members concerning an embarrassment caused by her husband. Mosa told them all that she knew nothing, she told them that she will explain after talking to her husband. He at that time switched his phone off and had gone into hiding as he was nowhere to be found. Mmamoruti and the other Bogosi uncles got on their cars and came to visit. Mosa was not surprised by their visit but it was useless as their son was not home and Mosa told them how he normally went into hiding every time he was in trouble. To the elders surprise Mosa confirmed it not to be the first time it happened and she told them how she was not even shocked because it was how their son lived. She told them everything even about the drugs. They were shocked as she continued to share the details of her marriage. Mmamoruti nearly fainted to the news that her nephew had turned into a monster who beats his wife and cheats on her with young girls. The Bogosi elders where in so much dismay that they asked Mosa why she did not get him arrested but got disgusted with the answer. It was as if some of the stories were made up but fortunately for Mosa she had a witness called Lorraine.

After a few days waiting for Richard to return home his family members decided to pack it up and retreat back to Bridgeville. They tried to convince Mosa to leave with them but she rejected their offer and told them she was staying in her marriage for the sake of her children. Mmamoruti sore to return as soon as Richard got back and promised to sort him out. Two weeks passed after they left before Richard returned home like nothing happened. As soon as he arrived Mosa signalled Loraine to call Mmamoruti and inform her. She woke them up the next morning ready to sort Richard out. Little did she know that the older Richard and the Richard she raised and knew years ago were two different people? She mistook the new Richard for the old sweet little boy she brought up and surprisingly she was way out of her league. Before she could even open her mouth to talk to Richard he threw her out of his house. He told her how his parents died in an accident and nobody could tell him what to do and when to do it. Mmamoruti left Richetown shocked and really worried about how things were going to be for Mosa. She arrived in Bridgeville and the first thing she did was call a family meeting. At that meeting the decision was made to arrange a meeting with the Paledi family as soon as possible because what Mmamoruti saw made her feel scared for Mosa and the children's lives. She was rightfully scared as that night Richard questioned Mosa why Mmamoruti was there and when she explained how the Bogosi uncles visited for days and left because he was not there. He asked her what she told them and when she replied that she told them everything, he burned with fury. Mosa left him in the bedroom and went to lie down on the couch in the lounge. He followed her there and he was cursing like there was no tomorrow. As Mosa tried to get away from him again, he pulled and hit her in the face with a fist so hard, Mosa fell to the floor. She tried to crawl and call Loraine for help but he stopped her by stepping on top of her with one foot, strangled her to stop her from screaming. She felt helpless and just lied there as he kicked her, hit her and doing whatever he liked with her; she did not even cry just took the kicks and beatings to her body until she lost consciousness, he saw that she was silence so he shook her violently hoping that she would wake up. He checked her pulse by putting his finger on her neck and the moment he realised that she was still alive, just fainted. He left her lying on that cold tilled floor, jumped her and went to the bedroom to sleep. Mosa lied there in her blood the whole night and was found by Lorraine the next morning. She called the ambulance and got her rushed to the hospital where she got resuscitated. Lorraine stayed home and took care of the children. When Richard woke up at ten o' clock he asked where his wife was as if nothing happened. Lorraine took the children to the room to prevent them from hearing her tell Richard that Mosa was lying in a hospital bed in a comma. Lorraine continued to tell him how she found Mosa passed out on the floor covered in blood and with her clothes torn. It was as if Richard had too characters; the monster and the loving husband and it was as if he switched them every minute. He stood up from where he was sited and rushed to the hospital. He ran before Loraine could tell her she called both the families. When he arrived at the hospital he found members from both the families. His aunt {Mmamoruti} took a phone and called the police on him. Richard got arrested at the hospital and what shocked the elders was when they went home that night they found Richard helping Lorraine by feeding their third child faith. For the first time the children felt the warmth and love from their father. He apologised to them and promised to change. He also agreed to seek help and professional assistance with his anger. He visited his wife in hospital until she woke up from a comma but Mosa was so angry at him she did not respond even when he was trying to apologise. All she did was cry. He did not give up and all the time Mosa was in hospital he became a parent to the children who longed to have him love them for a very long time or ever since birth for some of them. He bathed them, played with them even bonded with them. Mosa stayed in hospital for a month and three weeks and just as she was about to be discharged the doctor told her she was pregnant with her fourth child. Mosa cried uncontrollably when she heard that she was carrying a child of rape as she played back every moment of the day before she landed in hospital. The doctor advised her to get counselling as she seemed too traumatised. The counselling helped and Mosa returned home to her children. At that time Mmamoruti and one of Mosa's aunts were given the task of staying with them to monitor Richard's behaviour. During the days when the two aunts were staying at their house Richard became a model husband. He helped with the children, took them to school and spent time with them. The aunts got convinced that he was changed and left them when Mosa was five months pregnant. They went home and reported that there was peace in Richard and Mosa's home. The peace lasted for a while after Richard apologised for nearly killing her and for forcing himself on her. She forgave him and they went on with their lives.

All went well in the Bogosi family, Richard became the loving husband Mosa longed for and missed for a very long time. She was getting used to the idea of a happy marriage and she was getting comfortable with that. The model husband was supportive, went to the antenatal clinic with his wife. He was even in the hospital room when their fourth child was born. He even cut the umbilical cord and named their son Paul. Mosa happily brought the baby home with the help of her husband who genuinely seemed to have changed. Richard was in the mode which when somebody was to look at him, he would seem like the old and loving man was back.

It is true when they say a leopard cannot change its spots. When little Paul was three months old, Richard began his mischievous ways again. It was as if he was bewitched all over again. He invited his friend and colleagues to his house but gave Mosa strict instructions to keep the children locked in the back room until his party was over. The party was hosted at their house for the first time and it was only because the person who was supposed to host it, pulled out at short notice so Richard was forced to host it. According to him he never wanted any of his colleagues or associates to meet or see his wife and children. For some reason it was as if he was ashamed of his wife and children. He did not want people to know that they existed, he avoided entertaining at his house because he did not want people to meet them. His explanation to Mosa was that he was protecting them from the media. Mosa saw the little flashes of the old Richard reoccurring bit by bit. He started sleeping out again but he had not reached a stage where he beat her yet.it had not reached boiling point yet. He started cursing again, it was as if he was bewitched and this time the level was raised. He started to show signs of two characters again. He showed signs of drug use again and on top of that he was now having affairs with young women. He got worse to the point that he even brought them to his home. He would at that time bring a young girl into their matrimonial bedroom, wake his wife from their bed and make her watch as he commits adultery. The following morning he left with his young thing without a care in the world. Sometimes he would come late at night, bring along one of his concubines and on the same bed when his wife refused to jump off the bed and give them space; they would continue with whatever they were doing right next to her in the same bed. Mosa went through it all silently and she most of the time would spend trying to explain to his eleven year old son why a different young woman would leave their bedroom every morning or why they were still staying with their father. Mosa held on to a dying marriage while Richard was busy abusing her again and again. This time it got worse because he wanted to prevent Mosa from talking to people and forbade her from getting out of the gate. He hired the driver to take the children to school and bring them back. Mosa was ordered to write a grocery list and the driver was to do shopping for her even sanitary requirements. She was not allowed to go out not even to the hair salon, the hairdresser came to the house and did her hair. When she had a doctor's appointment he came to check her in the house. Richard had an excuse for everything he did to her. He stopped her from visiting his and her family as she was going to tell tales. All that time Mosa held, kept praying and hoping that God will one day change the situation and in the meantime she was busy coming up with a plan. She started a relationship with the driver and played the guilt trip because the driver noticed the kind of life she was living and became sympathetic towards her. He helped her because she told him that the abuse was happening the second time she was planning her exit out of the marriage. She became very close to the driver and made an arrangement for the driver to transfer money into her private account from her husband's bank account every week whenever he went to do grocery shopping. Mosa started hacking into her husband's internet banking and transferring money into her account on a weekly basis and because he was not observant he did not even care how his money was spent. Mosa would ask the driver to not only transfer money but she asked him to withdraw a certain amount every time he was sent shopping. Mosa told him she wanted a stash to can be able to pay for her transport should need arise. The driver was willing to help because he knew how his boss treated his wife. The driver and the maid were both concerned at how Richard would insult his wife in their presence. They were worried because Mosa would tell them that she was going to leave her husband but to them it seemed very difficult or even impossible as they knew the kind of man their boss was.

Richard did it all until he pulled the last straw on one cloudy night. As usual he arrived home at around seven o clock with a young woman in his arm. At that time Mosa and Lorraine were busy feeding the children. He came in holding a young woman's waist and it looked as if he was drunk. Mosa came out of the kitchen and greeted them. Richard called her and ordered her to greet the young lady with a special greeting, Mosa looked at the girl from toe to head and at that time she had enough. The cup of her anger had run over and all the evil man did to her had now come to an overflow. She replied and said to him: NO!, and then she left to continue feeding her children. Richard stood from the couch and went to the dining table, he asked Mosa what she just said to him in the presence of the guest. Mosa angrily said to him: "NO" I SAID NO!! That day after a very long time he slapped her across the face with the back of his hand so hard she fell. He did that in front of the children and their first born son stood from his chair and screamed "NO DAD, STOP IT! Richard slapped the little boy with the same hand he fell on top of his mother. The two middle children cried and he screamed at them saying: "BE QUIET, BE QUIET! YOU USELESS THINGS. The children cried even more and Lorraine just went into a frozen state. She was shaking like a leaf. The young woman on the couch became so scared she did not even know whether to run away or stay. She was also shocked. Richard came back from the bathroom and found Mosa trying to comfort the children as they were crying very loud, Lorraine was in the kitchen bringing food for Thato and Joy when she heard him shout "TAKE YOUR CHILDREN AND GET OUT OF MY HOUSE NOW!' she came out running and found Richard locking the front door with Mosa and the children outside. She was speechless. The unknown lady tried to speak but Richard signalled her with his hand to shut it. The children and Mosa were sitting on the porch, they were still crying so Richard came out, went to the gate and opened the gate for them and ordered them out. The rain was drizzling and as the kids had just bathed and because all that happened suddenly and unexpectedly, they were only dressed in sleeping clothes. Mosa tried to beg Richard and plead for their sakes but he threw them all out of the gate and locked it. Mosa covered her children as they sat on the front lawn. The children stopped crying instead they were shocked at the fact that the rain was pouring on their heads but it was as if they would rather be in that rainy and peaceful place than be with the devil dressed as a father. Mosa only realised the children's reaction and was shocked that they were aware of what was happening, they just were too young to have helped her. The poor woman and her children sat on the lawn in front of their yard with the rain falling on them and they had nowhere to go. The rain became strong by the minute and it was falling hard on them. Mosa closed her eyes and said a silent prayer as she did not want her children to know that she was praying for God to save her children. Her tears rolling on her cheeks were mixed with the rain waters, she cried silently, trying so hard to hide it so her children would not notice that she was in pain, crying, praying and pleading for mercy upon their lives from God. At that time it was not even possible to walk anywhere because it was dark and all she thought of was the safety of her children so they sat on the wet lawn with the hope that by some miracle their father will grow a heart, realised how strong the rain was and maybe sympathise on them. That never happened in fact they saw all the lights of the house getting switched off; even the outside lights which were normally left on for security reasons. On that day they were all switched off as if he knew that they were on the front lawn, in front the security wall. The darkness brought a moment of silence and a few questions to a mother who was protecting her children. She wished to have a nest which was comfortable enough to just protect her children until night and that cruel rain came to a dead end which at that time seemed to be dragging. It is true that God will never leave nor forsake his children. During that moment when she was desperately seeking the hand of God, his divine intervention or maybe even a sign that God heard the prayers of a destitute woman who was fearing for both her life and that of her children in a bad situation. She closed her eyes and spoke to God in her heart, pleaded for God to show her a miracle by saving her children. She prayed that none of her children catch a flu or even sickness from the rain which was pouring very hard on them. Her silent prayer was one which she just touched the heart of God in heaven as while she was busy praying she saw a bright light shine in through the covered cups of her closed eyes. She slowly opened her eyes and found bright lights of a car, which were directed at her and the children. The children were also quiet and shocked as they had spent about two hours in the dark, cold and rainy weather. They all watched to see who would come out of the light from that vehicle and out of it came the front opposite neighbour Mrs Smith, who came out of the car running and took them into her house. They were dripping wet and she gave them towels to dry up, she looked in her cupboards and gave them dry clothes. Even though they were a bigger size for the children, it was better that nothing. They were shaking from the cold and she made them something warm to drink. She gave them food just before she rushed out to a seven eleven store. She came back with diapers, baby formula and baby food. Luckily by that time Paul was still asleep. Mosa told Mrs Smith how grateful she was that she took them in. she thanked her for all she did for her and her children. They put the children to sleep just before they sat and for the first time in many years; Mosa shared the story of her life with a stranger. She told her where they came from and how they ended in Richetown. She told her everything that Richard did to her and finished by telling her that he had just pulled a last stunt and that she was leaving for Stoneville in the morning. Mrs Smith was shocked at how much the poor woman had to take. She agreed with her that it was either she takes the children back home or she was going to end dead, killed by her husband. Mrs Smith told Mosa that it really was surprising how long Mosa lasted under those difficult conditions. They went to sleep with Mosa tossing and turning all night. She kept playing a movie of all the years of heartache and abuse she had to take. She also remembered who and what her young and handsome love was towards her. All that was a journey of her heart erasing every part of the good that Richard was to her and replacing it with all the pain and hurt which had occurred and converted every inch of her soul into a drum sounding only offense and plans of revenge. That night she kept up a good struggle with very strange but understandable feelings of hate and rage as they filled her heart with thoughts of how to avenge her life and that of her defenceless children. She continuously stopped her mind from thinking thoughts which came to her; telling her to either go back to that house and steal her husband's gun and clean out all the rounds on his chest, some thought were for her to play the submissive and just when he relaxes to the idea that she forgave him; she was to serve him a meal and a drink which were to finally quicken his journey to his creator. The night seemed to have brought her bad ideas which she combated by a blessing of a good heart that God had given to her. Through it all she kept having a voice telling her that she was to remember the word of God which told her that "Vengeance is mine" says the Lord. That scripture did its job on that night because after all the sweet and sour memories; she made peace and thanked God for sending her neighbour at the right time when she needed her the most.

The next morning Mrs Smith called her work and took the day off. She wanted to offer Mosa all the help she needed. Because Mosa had told her how Richard bribed his way out of everything they concluded that Mosa had no choice but to return to her maternal home. Mrs Smith helped Mosa call her children's school and explain everything to the principal who was so understanding that she immediately made arrangements for the kids to go to a new school in Stoneville. She helped and told Mosa to only worry about their safety, she promised to let her know when they arrived in Stoneville. When all that was done Mosa asked Mrs Smith to look after the children as she went to her house. She knew the driver was supposed to come and collect the children for school because he had no idea what had happened. As soon as she came out of the gate the driver opened her house gate trying to enter. Mosa got into the car and told Pule what happened the previous night. Pule was shocked and Mosa told him to pretend he knew nothing. They went into the house with his keys and found Richard drinking coffee. The young lady was seated on the couch were Mosa left her the previous night. It looked as though she slept there. Richard stood from the chair and approached them, he greeted Pule and looked at Mosa as he asked her: what do you want? She replied and said; I want our clothes and things for the baby. He arrogantly said to her, Beg Me! With shock she said what? He turned and said, are you deaf? I said Beg Me! She said to him; for our children's sake I beg you, please grant me permission to take their clothes as they are dressed in night clothes. He came a few steps closer and ordered her to be on her knees. All this happened while Pule was watching and seemed disgusted at what was happening. Mosa got on her knees and began to beg again. He took steps closer to her and said: Lick My Shoes! Mosa looked up in shock and screamed, what? He repeated and said: Lick My Shoes! Pule tried to stop him but he signalled him with his hand to say nothing. The young girl on the couch stood and screamed; Stop it, Stop it, didn't you humiliate her enough yesterday? He turned and said to her; Shut up, or Get out. She stormed out and said to him:

66

God will punish you for this! Richard turned his attention to Mosa and told her to continue with what he ordered her to do. Mosa's tears rolled from her eyes in her heart she wanted access to the bedroom where she had cash and bank cards hidden. She said something out loud while crying: I am doing this for my children and I will do it over and over again. She bowed her head and leaked his shoes with Pule holding his hand over his eyes not to watch. Richard took a few steps back and took of one of his shoes. He smelled it, put it back on, and kicked them in her direction. He cursed her and said: NOW MY SHOES SMELL! THEY SMELL OF YOUR POVERTY STRIKKEN BREATH. He put both the shoes in front of her and yelled: You can have them, they are yours, use them to buy you and your grandmother a better house, because the price of those shoes alone can buy a house for her and feed your entire family for the rest of your lives. The helpless woman continued to listen as he continued to curse her and her poverty stricken family. He insulted her so much after giving her the shoes. The poor woman was still on the floor with tears rolling out of her eyes and Pule standing next to her feeling very helpless. She cried her lungs out, shaking on her knees and painfully sobbing like never before and Pule could not move or even make a sound. Richard came back and ordered her to go into the house and clean herself up. He also told her to take whatever she needed. She went in and as she was busy washing the blood off her nose and wiping her tears. Richard gave Pule the keys to one of their SUV and told him to drive Mosa wherever she wanted to go. The condition was he was to report to Richard all the movements. As usual Richard told him that he had to rush to the meeting somewhere and he left him standing there after asking him where Lorraine was. Pule did not even know where Lorraine was so he went into the backroom to check on her. He found there with all her bags packed. She asked him if there was anybody in the house. He told him what had just happened and she confirmed the details of what happened the previous night. She told him that her bags are packed and she was going back home and was never returning to that house again. She told him that she could not take what was going on anymore. She also said Mr Richard was going to kill her madam and she did not want to witness that. Pule told Lorraine that Madam was packing and that time she was leaving. Lorraine went into the big house and said her goodbyes and Mosa; told her that she was also leaving. Lorraine commended her, begged her not to ever return and that was if she wanted to continue to live and see her children grow. Mosa thanked her two employees for their support and loyalty as they said their goodbyes and told them she was going back to her home in Stoneville. While Mosa was busy telling them that she got stopped by Pule who told her that Richard left in a hurry and gave him the keys to an SUV. He also told Pule to take Mosa wherever she wanted to go. They concluded that he thought she was going to need medical attention because of a broken nose and at that time it was a blessing that he did not even think of calling a doctor for her like he normally did or it was because he was in the second character mode which was loving and remorseful and that was the reason he told him to drive her anywhere she wanted to go.

Mosa asked Pule if he still had the petrol card and he said yes. Finding that out she told Pule about her plan; which was for him to take advantage of the offer and drive them back to Stoneville. Pule gladly agreed to drive Mosa and the children to Stoneville and just as Lorraine was about to leave, Mosa paid her from her hidden stash of cash and also paid Pule money for driving them. She ordered him to pack all the bags in the car while she ran to Mrs Smith's house to get the children. When she got there she thanked her Good Samaritan for saving her and the children. Mrs Smith was only happy that they were getting out of the lion's den called Mosa's marriage. They said their goodbyes and after a change of clothes Mosa took her children and when they got to their house they found the car fully packed and ready to drive off. They left at about half past ten with Mosa saying in her heart; I am not coming back to this house no matter what.

Ten

They travelled to Stoneville and arrived at around two o clock in the afternoon and all they were glad about was how they had a smooth and comfortable ride. After Pule offloaded the car he asked for the room to rest and he asked Mosa to wake him up after two hours. Mmaleuba and Mosa's siblings were not surprised to see them coming home in the middle of the week and when it was not even school holidays. The old woman knew that Richard has happened, she saw by their luggage; and the expression on the children's faces that it meant they were there to stay. Mosa woke Pule up after two hours and gave him food to eat before he left for Richetown. They said their goodbyes and he left.

After he left Mosa sat down her family members and narrated the story to the point of them ending up in Stoneville. Mmaleuba saw that her granddaughter was beat down emotionally. She just welcomed her and told her how she was glad that Mosa and the children were alive. She told Mosa to try very hard to forgive her husband because that way she was going to be able to move on with her life. Mercy spoke out of turn and said: I won't get married, if married people suffer like my sister did then I don't want to get married. Mmaleuba reprimanded her but she was partly write. The truth of the matter was there used to be a trend which was showing in that family. Mmaleuba's husband had left her, he returned home very sick and weak, ready to die without a cent to his name. The second one was Mosa's mom who had no luck with men until she married the monster who abused her and kept her away from her children. Now it was Mosa who thought she had a happily ever after; but only to get a monster husband who cursed like there was no tomorrow, who turned her into his punching bag immediately after he made it in the big time, how he turned her into a baby making machine and completely forgot his promises to make her a gospel star. He abused her so much he even forgot that she could sing. He controlled her so much, he forgot that she was human with real feelings. If that was not a pattern then what was? The last words Mosa said were she was going to return to her matrimonial home only over her dead body. She went into the rooms and took out of one of her bags a pair of expensive Italian shoes and told them how she got herself a souvenir from her dead marriage that morning. She showed them the blood which was still on the shoes and told them it was hers. She told them that those shoes were a confirmation that it was finally over between her and Richard and she did not care how rich he was. She said she would rather stay poor but happy and alive than die rich and unhappy. All agreed with her. The phone call was made to the Bogosi family by Mmaleuba who narrated the new developments that happened to their children's marriage. Luckily for Mosa; she had reported Richard countless times to them and truth be told, the families failed to control the situation. As they were also born again Christians, one would have thought that they would be against divorce but in that case they agreed that Mosa should have left Richard a long time. They agreed that until Richard came to them and asked for their assistance in getting his wife back home, Mosa was to stay in Stoneville but as both the families believed that God hates divorce she was told not to file for one and wait in hope that God was the one to turn her marriage situation around. Mosa was a humble woman, she listened to her in-laws and abided by their advice. All she did was pray and trusted God that he was faithful to fight her battles on her behalf.

Back in Richetown Pule kept going to the house in the morning and in the afternoons. He did that for a whole week and after that he called Mosa and told her that Richard had disappeared and no one saw or heard from him in the last seven days. Mosa was not even shocked because he always disappeared after causing trouble, in that case he left immediately after kicking a shoe at his wife's nose and after seeing her bleed he got struck by guilt, he told the driver to drive her wherever she wanted to go and he made that offer because he felt regretful. That made him afraid of the fact that he offended his wife and his fear of him getting arrested had caused him to go into hiding. Mosa told Pule that he was only into hiding and he should eventually show up. She instructed Pule to get in the house at night and switch the light on and come back the next morning to switch them off and water the plants as no one stayed in the house. Pule continued to take care of the house for three weeks until Richard came back from wherever he had gone. He had no idea that his wife, children and maid left on the same day he disappeared. They had already moved on with their lives without him. The children were even settled in their new school. They were attending counselling and were getting their lives back to normal.

He came to the house as usual shouting: honey, I am home! He entered and found his driver seated on the couch and said: "you are not my wife", where is my wife? He asked that as if he didn't know what happened the day he left. Pule replied him by saying: they are in Stoneville Sir. Ha! Where? He exclaimed. Stoneville Sir.

Pule repeated. How? When she had no money, I made sure I took all the bank cards in the house, so how did she get to Stoneville? He asked. Pule replied him by saying: but you gave me a petrol card Sir, and told me to drive her wherever she wanted to go. She told me to drive her and the kids to Stoneville Sir. He angrily said to Pule that he told him to drive her to the doctor as she was injured and not to Stoneville. He took back the keys to his car and his petrol card and gave Pule a few days off. He told him to come back after a week to collect his salary. Before Pule left he asked him where Lorraine was and he only realised the house was empty when Pule confirmed that Lorraine also quit her job. He stayed in the house for a week, without cleaning, he would wake up, go to work and return home with some take-away food. He would eat the food and pile up his dirt without cleaning. The day that Pule came to collect his month's salary he had nowhere to sit let alone Richard, who could not even walk as rubbish was pilled everywhere. He paid Pule his money and asked him to help find a new maid for the house. Pule brought three ladies to clean the mess the next morning and after the house was cleaned he hired one of them to work there regularly. Her name was Cate. Richard thanked Pule and rehired him back to his driver position. He realised that Pule was very helpful and he cared for the house more than he could so he even offered him a position as a house manager. His reasons were that the children were no longer driven by Pule but he still needed a job and seeing that Richard was driving himself; Pule's job was to manage the house, make sure that all was done properly. He was just hiding the fact that he realised that Pule was the only person who kept him company because his life was lonely and slowly becoming miserable without his wife and children in that house. The irony was he was just unbelievable. When they were in his house he was abusing and not appreciating them but at that time someone would have thought he missed them even if he had disappeared for such a long time without a care about how his absence was affecting them. They spent a lot of time together and meanwhile, just because he respected Mosa and had hope for their marriage or maybe out of loyalty for the both of them, looking at the fact that he was employed by that family for more than twelve years, Pule kept reporting everything to Mosa. What was surprising was she did not even care about Richard and what went on in his live but she kept taking the reports even if the information was useless to her.

Just as expected from a promiscuous Richard, he never called his wife, not even to check how the children were doing. He was busy hiding the fact that he misses them behind a bottle of expensive whisky or a sniff of cocaine which he called recreational to help him sleep at night. The other thing which kept him from calling was he knew that the families were involved in the matter and it meant he had to sit down with them to ask for his wife to return back and because he was arrogant, he did not contact them. He just stopped caring the minute he realised they were not returning home. Even though he never tried he knew that it was going to be a struggle to win his family back, remembering all he did and put them through. After six weeks Richard filled for a divorce without consulting Mosa. He was wrongly advised by the men who he used to sit, drink and talk rubbish with. One of them advised him to file for divorce and that way Mosa was to come back running to him fearing that it will come true. Little did the man know that he was indeed filling Richard's head with an evil plan to get rid of his wife and children for good so he could freely live his dirty life?

He got help from one of his corrupt friends who worked at the court and only called Mosa to hear if the papers had been couriered or hear if she received them. He called and when Mosa picked the call Hello; he said: how are you? Mosa said; I am fine. And the children? He asked. They are fine, Mosa answered. And the school? He asked. Mosa angrily answered him by saying: my children are in school. He said ok but Mosa impatiently asked him how she could be of assistance to him. He told her how he was checking if she received the divorce papers. Mosa nearly fainted, she asked him to repeat what he just said. He said: yes, I have filled for a divorce and I called to check if you received the papers. He told her the hearing was set for a date two months from that day on. After Mosa caught her breath, she said to Richard; whatever you want from me Sir I will do. He told her to expect the papers as he had them couriered. She thanked him for the warning and he arrogantly told her he was giving her exactly what she wanted. Mosa realised that he was provoking her so she just hung the phone.

She immediately told her grandmother that Richard filled for a divorce. Mmaleuba was shocked and she comforted Mosa by saying that she was the one who was supposed to have filled for a divorce a long time ago. Mosa reminded her granny that the word of God said in Malachi chapter 2 verse 16(NIV) "I the Lord God of Israel hates divorce." Her granny spoke against her and said: the same Malachi chapter 2 verse 1 up to verse 15(NIV) says that God becomes angry when a man marries a wife of his youth and abuses her. That opened a debate until Mosa told her granny that the papers had been filled and there was nothing she or any family member could do about it. She told her that the comfort to all was she was not the one filling for a divorce. She added by saying that she knew for a fact that by then Richard did not want her back. Mmaleuba made a call to Bridgeville to report the latest. The Bogosi had nothing left to do but only to promise Mosa their support through it all. They also promised to help Mosa by forcing their son to maintain his children. Mmaleuba agreed that her granddaughter deserved support as she was not the one in the wrong. The confirmation of the divorce came two weeks later. Mosa knew that it was really over between her and Richard.

Because Mosa and the children were used to living a good life. They ate certain foods and had a very peculiar taste. She had a secret savings account which she opened while she was planning her Exit out of Richard's life. She also had some cash which she collected from Pule on a regular basis every time he went shopping for them since she was caged in the house by her husband. All the money was slowly running out as Mosa was trying to keep the standard of life for her children the same way as they used to live in Richtown. She kept her hope that Richard will maybe pay her a divorce settlement and also thought that he was going to pay maintenance following the court instructions. Her recourses were busy running dry and her only hope was in the court as she could not even afford to hire a lawyer as she was unemployed and it seemed very difficult even for her to walk down the streets, let alone job hunting. She was still feeling ashamed by the fact that she was the one who had the biggest and beautiful wedding in their village and now she was back from her marriage and for good. She kept wondering how long it would take busybodies like Meiki to come knocking at her granny's door just to ask why the children were now attending school in Stoneville. It was difficult for her even to go to the nearest tuck shop just to buy bread as she was uncertain of whom she will meet along the way and what questions they would ask her. For the first few weeks she experienced a few signs of depression, closed the door of her room but the love for her children drove her out as she had to walk them to school sometimes if their uncle was not around to do it. After receiving a call from her estranged husband, she just gained strength and started preparing for the divorce hearing which was too close according to her.

Pule and his wife Ouma were kind enough to offer Mosa a place to stay for a period while she was attending their divorce hearing. She left their children with her sister and other family members on the eighth of May. It was a cold winter afternoon when she said her goodbyes and left for Johannesburg promising her children to be back with lots of goodies for them. Mmaleuba promised to pray for her trip to be successful. She arrived there and was grateful to Pule and his wife for accommodating her. That morning Pule drove her to court as he was still Richard's house manager and a car he drove belonged to Richard so he saw it fit to help her before he went to work. He was more loyal to Mosa as he had seen her go through a lot in her marriage. He dropped her off at court earlier so Mosa waited outside the room which number was the same as the one written on the papers she had. She waited for an hour and thirty minutes and while she was seated there Richard came in and walked in the room, holding hands with another young woman. She watched in dismay and disgusted she just kept her cool and remained on that bench outside of that room. After thirty minutes a man came out and called Mosa in. She was actually surprised to see that there was someone in the room because ever since she was there no one entered that room except for Richard and his toy. That made her wonder why they entered the room and why they spent such a long time in that room without her. She came in but her gut instinct kept getting a suspicion that something was going on. She entered the room and greeted them. The strange man asked her if she had a lawyer and she said: no. she further explained how she had no idea that she needed a lawyer as it was the first day of the hearing. The man shocked Mosa further by saying to her that it was not necessary to bring a lawyer anyway as the conclusion was that since Richard was the only one working throughout their marriage he was to get everything. She expressed her shock by saying; oh! Really? And the children? Richard arrogantly jumped in and said: No, No, No, No, you keep them they are all yours. Mosa asked again; and maintenance? He replied her and said; I don't have money for that, besides I can't maintain them if they stay with you and your family. He continued and said: "maybe you should get a job and see how it feels to work a day in your life." The man stood from a chair holding papers in her hand and said to Richard:" be quiet, I will handle this" he then approached Mosa and said to her presenting her with the papers: "all we need is your signature" Mosa asked with tears in her eyes: oh! So this is why I came all the way from Stoneville? The man said to Mosa: lady can you afford a lawyer? With what? Mosa angrily replied. The man said to Mosa that she had no lawyer and that meant she won't be able to have a say in court. Mosa knew nothing about divorce hearings and all the procedures and she realised that her criminal of a husband had just crooked and cheated her out of everything. The man pressurised her so much she saw that she was left with no choice but to sign the papers. She signed the papers with tears rolling from her eyes, her hands were shaking. She was in so much pain she felt like she was going to vomit. It felt to her like someone called Richard just punched her very hard in the stomach. The man said to Mosa that she will receive the decree of divorce by courier soon. She asked the man: are we done? And the man after checking every page and making sure if she signed and initialled everything, he said: yes, we are done. Mosa went out the room and Richard followed with his girlfriend. She stopped them and said to him: can you at least give money for the children. He said arrogantly: "hello! Didn't you get the memo? We are divorced baby! They are your responsibility now, not mine. Mosa asked him again: and now that we are divorced, how am I supposed to get back to Stoneville? You got my signature now how do I get back to my home because you know very well that I have nothing? He took out his purse and threw three hundred rants at Mosa's face, the money fell on the ground and he said; "that should be enough, now don't bother me again. He took his girlfriend as they left giggling.

The poor woman bowed down to pick the money from the floor and she could not stand up, she cried hysterically. Her body went into shock and she was alone without anybody to help her. She crawled to the nearest bench and there she cried silently but uncontrollably. It was like she was just having a nightmare and she could wake up any minute from it, but it was not true. The reality of her marriage crushing down hit her like a ton of bricks. She had just experienced day light robbery at the hand of her love, the only man she ever devoted herself to. Her one and only true lover just twisted the knife and left it there. It felt to her as though the world just became different for her. She felt dizzy, as if she would faint any minute. She was sweating and hyperventilating. That lasted for about forty five minutes until she calmed herself up. Meanwhile as Pule was coming out of the shop at a mall not far from the court, he saw his Mr Richard celebrating with his new found friend. They were sitting at a restaurant clicking glasses and laughing from ear to ear. He just sensed there and then that it meant trouble for Mosa. He checked his cell phone for missed calls and found that she had not called. Something just told him to go and check for her at court. He found her trying very hard to collect her emotions but as soon as she saw him, she cried uncontrollably again. She could not even control herself. Pule tried to take her to the car but she refused and said, "it's not mine" I can't" he is, I hate! She was just hysterical and Pule was unable to make sense of all her utterings because she could not even finish sentences. With his gentle nature, he kept saying can we just get inside the car, "ALL WILL BE WELL MY SISTER" He supported her to the car and she would not get in. He also felt helpless. After a long struggle he managed to get her into the car and drove her to his home. On his way he called his wife who was at work and asked if she could get permission for leaving work early because he realised that moment; the situation was beyond him. As it is normally said "IT WAS NOT RAINING, IT WAS POURING". She came back from work and found her husband worried because Mosa was hysterical she could not even talk. He told his wife how he saw his master celebrating with one of his young concubines, and immediately got the feeling something went completely wrong. He went to court and checked on Mosa only to find her in a state. He also told her how Mosa was refusing to get into the car even though they agreed that he was supposed to pick her up after the hearing.

Ouma made her some sugar water and forced her to drink it. She drank it and after a while she was calm and able to talk. She started telling them all that happened to her at court. They were shocked to a point that Pule decided to tell his wife that enough was enough. He had been looking for another job for a while but at that time he did not find anything. He there and then decided to take back

Richard's car and resign. He did not even consider the consequences. Pule said to them that he would rather die of hunger than to work for a ruthless man who stole everything from his wife of many years and children. He agreed with his wife that there was no turning back. Mosa asked them to consider their options before they make a drastic decision. They both told her that there was no turning back. She thanked them for their support and loyalty.

Pule took the car and left while Mosa and Ouma continued talking. Ouma asked Mosa if she was going to really use the R300 that Richard gave to her to go back to Stoneville. Mosa told her she was considering the fact that she had no place to stay. She said that even if she stayed in Richetown where would she find a job? She also told her that she was dreading the part where she had to face her children and tell them that their father does not want them. They spoke and while their conversation continued Ouma remembered that she heard of a woman in the suburbs where she was working who was looking for a domestic worker to work two days a week. Ouma just brought it forward but Mosa jumped and said to her: I`ll take it, please take me there. She calmed her and said to her they were to go the next morning. She told Ouma that she chooses to be a domestic worker than to go through the shame of telling her family what Richard did to her. They got stopped by Pule walking in as he just got off the taxi. He came in and told them how when he got there and before he could say anything he was fired for transporting Mosa to and from court. Apparently the same man who Richard paid to speed up the divorce procedure saw Pule helping Mosa into the car. He immediately called Richard and reported Pule and as he went there he found Richard burning with fury. He fired him, took his car keys and gave him three months' salary as his severance pay. Mosa was shocked and she found herself uttering these words: "Richard is busy drawing the wrath of God to himself, he is going to get punished for what he did to me, and now for what he just did to you."

Eleven

Mosa went with Ouma the next day to speak to her prospective madam. Pule also went to the factories in search for a new job. They arrived at the suburbs and the madam told Mosa to work a day to prove that she was able to work, and after that she was going to tell her if she was hired or not. She worked very hard and at the end of that day she was offered the job and she was also told to come and assist with the cocktail party which her madam was hosting that following Saturday. She agreed and was very happy as she needed the extra money. She went to work that Tuesday, Thursday and even went to a cocktail party to work on Saturday.

At the cocktail party there were about fifty to sixty people. Mostly women who came from suburbs around Richetown. They were ordering Mosa around but fortunately for her not even one of them recognised her. That was all thanks to her husband who kept her like a caged animal and never allowed her to socialise with other women.

She worked very hard and impressed one of the ladies who offered her a job for the days of the week that she did not work. Mosa was very happy that she could now make enough money to send some for the children back home and have some left over for her to rent a room. She was just pleased with the fact that she never went home at least she was going be able to make ends meet. When she got home that night she shared the good news that she found more work and her friends were very happy for her judging by her circumstances.

She went to work on Monday morning and that night it was time to celebrate with Pule who also got a job at a nearby factory as a driver. They celebrated with leftovers from their jobs of roasted chicken, bread and a salad. They ate, sang, prayed and went to bed peacefully. The following morning Mosa went to start her second job at the new madam's house. That day went well and as her new madam whose name was Mary tried to find out more about Mosa she told her how she came from Stoneville and she told her about her four children who she left back home but she left out a lot of details. Mary had a feeling that Mosa was leaving out details of her life but she did not want to sound pushy and just kept accepting that which she was telling her. Mary kept asking questions until they discussed accommodation where Mosa told Mary that she was staying with friends but she was going to look for her own room at the end of that month. Mary realised that if Mosa had to pay for rent she was not going to have enough money to send her four children. She felt a sudden sympathy for her maid whom she knew only for a day. Her sympathy led to her offering Mosa her backroom to stay in rent free and she even told her the room had a bed. She told her that whatever they have for her they will give. Mosa was very grateful but before she could accept the offer Mary told her she had to discuss it with her husband first.

The story behind Mary and her husband was that they owned a recording studio but Mary never told Mosa about it. She only said that when her husband got back from work she was going to discuss letting Mosa stay in their back room. Gregory knew Richard as they were both in the music industry, Gregory's record label was struggling financial while Richard's label was flourishing. Gregory's investors even threatened to get out of their deal if he did not do anything to save his company. He was given a deadline to sign a big star who was going to make a name for his record label or else he was left with no choice but to close his doors. Mary worked as his part time secretary who sometimes worked from home and sometimes worked at the office. At that time Mr Gregory was trying very hard to find a star but it was difficult as competition was very tough and Richard was not making it easy for him as he was always signing new artists. For Gregory it was as if he was bewitched as he was also a good producer but it seemed as though his business just took a down turn and there was nothing good happening to it. He always had headaches from investors who were threatening him and busy dishing out ultimatums. That day he came back home and when his wife told her about helping Mosa out with a place to stay rent free, he agreed after hearing how his wife described Mosa's difficult life. They agreed that Mosa can be told on Wednesday which meant she was to move in their back room on Friday.

Mosa went back home to share the news with Pule and his wife that she might have found a room. She told them that she was going to hear from her new Madam on Wednesday which meant she might move in on Friday. Pule and Ouma were happy but sad at the same time that she was leaving their home. She thanked them for their hospitality and kindness. Pule advised her that she should at least tell her family about the new developments in her life. He told her that now that she had a full week's job it was better for her to tell her family that she was staying in Richetown so they won't think that she went back to Richard. She immediately called her sister and gave her the message for their granny. She told her that she will explain what happened in court when she arrived home. She explained to her that she found a job and promised to send money for the children at the end of the month. Rose promised her sister to take good care of her children and promised to report their progress now and then to her elder sister. Mosa sighed a sigh of relieve after hanging the line. She had just completed a difficult part of telling the people at home that she was not returning home. On Wednesday she went to work and Mary told her the good news, she got excited more by the fact that she was to stay there rent free. She went back and packed for moving in on Friday. On Thursday she went to work for Madam Lizzie and on Friday morning she said her goodbyes and left to stay and work in the suburbs. She continued to work for both houses for four months and sending money for the children every month but she only went home one weekend in one month. Mary and Gregory treated her so well she felt like she was part of their family.

Mosa loved singing and especially when she was cleaning. One day Gregory woke up not feeling well. He was struggling with the stress of not finding a big music star and it was causing him very strong headaches. That morning he felt very sick and they decided that he should drink some pills and sleep in as his wife went to the office. He drank the medication and his wife went to the office very early that morning. Mosa did not know that her boss was sleeping so as usual she sang at the top of her voice and woke Gregory up. She continued to sing and Gregory heard something he had been looking for for a very long time, the voice which put butterflies into one's stomach. The healing voice with a surprising edge to shake the hardest of hearts. The voice which sounded like that one of angels, cherubim's or even the heavenly Sinhandrin. A true and spirit filled worship. He realised that Mosa is the big star who can turn his record label around. He woke up and walked in to the room where Mosa was and she immediately stopped singing. She got on her knees and apologised and explained that she was not aware that Mr Gregory was still sleeping. Gregory told her how he felt sick in the morning but at that moment he was healed and he had to rush to the office. Mary got the surprise of her life when she saw her husband showing up at the office, full of life again. She was confused because normally Gregory used to have the constant headaches and he would lie in bed for days, but the Gregory she left at home in the morning was a totally different man. She kept asking herself questions as to whether her husband had found a solution to their financial trouble. She followed him into the office and Gregory told her what happened that morning. He told her that there was no doubt that Mosa was their way out of trouble. Mary was shocked that their maid can solve their financial problems. Gregory spoke to his wife until he convince her that she had to hear Mosa sing herself but also told her that Mosa was very shy and would never sing for Mary voluntarily. His wife got a bit surprised but he quickly told him that he only found and heard Mosa singing to her highest level of ability because she thought she was alone in their house. Mary realised and agreed that Mosa might be reluctant to sing if she was to confront her about that fact. Mary and Gregory came up with a plan to catch Mosa unaware because that was the only way she could sing comfortably. They came up with a plan where Mary told Mosa that she and her husband were going out for dinner one night. She planned everything to the last point. She gave Mosa dinner and told her they won't be home until late that night. She said that she was meeting her husband somewhere. Mosa was very relaxed as she prepared to have an early night. After hearing the car drive off she thought she was alone and started singing, praising and worshiping. At that time Mary was in the room close to Mosa's and listening in. she heard how amazing Mosa's voice was. She just found herself in tears. She just listened to how Mosa was hitting her high and low notes. It was like she was listening to a professional musician. She called her husband and she met him a few houses away from their house. They left for the restaurant and on their way there Mary told Gregory what she just heard. She told her husband how difficult it was to pull herself away from listening to that voice. They ate dinner and discussed a plan of how to approach Mosa. After pulling straws

Mary was the one who was left with the responsibility of talking to their maid.

Mary decided that morning to just grab a bull by the horns and asked Mosa what they were requesting from her. She started by telling Mosa where they worked and told her the truth that they were given six months to turn things around for the company or the investors were pulling out of the deal. She told her that they had only two months left to sign a big star who was to put their company back on the map. Mosa was so sympathetic she offered to do anything to help them. Mary caught her and told her they needed help from her indeed. Mosa was so excited to help the people who had mercy on her when she needed help. She jumped and said: how can I be of help? Mary said to her; by singing for us, she further explained to Mosa that they were probably going to offer her a recording deal without a signing fee, but before she could even finish explaining Mosa jumped literally from her chair and shouted! Me? How did you know I could sing? She was surprised but also excited about the offer. Mary confessed to Mosa all they did after the morning Gregory heard her sing. Mosa was left speechless. The conversation ended with Mosa telling Mary how she wanted time to think about the matter and promised to give them the answer by that same night when Gregory is home.

He came back home to the news that they have a meeting with Mosa who had to respond to their offer. She came in from the backroom and kept them in their misery just for a little longer. She delayed answering them but finally she said yes. They all jumped up for joy. They stayed all night discussing the strategy of how to hide Mosa's identity until the launch of her album. Gregory was very clever about it he wanted to create a hype around Mosa's album which was going to make people stand on their feet and wait in anticipation to see the face behind the song. They stopped Mosa from working as their maid but she refused and offered to help out in the house every time she was not in studio recording. Mary also reminded them that Mosa had to continue working for Lizzie to keep up her cover because they said if Lizzie was to find out she was going to spread the news like wild fire. In the suburb where she lived they called her 'Mrs News' she was known to be the one who knew everything about everybody. Mosa agreed to everything they said and to keep everything under wraps. She agreed to the secrecy for two reasons, one being she was nervous about the whole thing and did not want to be disappointed should it fail. The second reason was she respected her bosses and friends because they knew best. They all went to bed praying and hoping that all will go well.

Twelve

The G.M. music team started by working on one song for Gregory to present the faceless voice. He brushed up on his presentation and decided to keep Mosa's identity hidden. They worked day and night to perfect Mosa' song until all were satisfied with it. It was agreed that the song was a heat. They continued to work in secret as Gregory was determined to hide Mosa's identity but he was also more worried about his presentation to the investors. The day of the presentation arrived where Mary and Mosa spent it praying for all to go well. He presented it to his investors and they unanimously approved after countless tries and he had been failing to impress them. The voice of Mosa made it easy for all the investors to give Gregory a go ahead plus they even agreed to a faceless voice tactic. They were very happy with him and for the first time the meeting ended in laughter. Gregory came home and also played the suspense game. They nearly killed him with screams when he shared the news that the meeting was successful. He also told them how Mosa's voice clinched the deal. They even signed off on Mosa's signing fee. As Gregory handed over the cheque to Mosa she could not believe how much money was written on that piece of paper. He told her that the real job had just began.

Gregory ran away with promoting Mosa's album and by the grace of God he succeeded with all the radios he went to and the song was even played on televisions as an advertisement for the launch. The song got played so much that people wanted to see the face behind the wonderful and amazing voice. All everybody anticipated was the day of the revelation which was advertised. The country went wild with the song and everybody was singing one song and kept asking for more. In all and with all that happening Gregory and his wife still did not know the true identity of their star. They only knew her to be Mosa Leuba from Stoneville who was their domestic worker and soon to be saviour with an angelic voice. The truth got revealed after an invitation list was drawn for all the very important guests and Mosa was given the list to add the people she wanted to invite. She added only three people, her sister Rose as it was for financial reasons that more members of her family would travel from Stoneville to attend her album launch even though they wished to join them, Pule and his wife Ouma. She wrote and as she perused through the list she saw the name of Richard Bogosi and nearly fainted. The list fell from her shaking hands to the floor and as Mary and her husband looked at her shocked state, and also in total dismay, she ran to the back room crying, locked herself in the room and cried so much because she was busy reminding herself of everything Richard put her through. Gregory and Mary were left wondering what they did wrong to anger Mosa in that way. In the back room Mosa felt it was fair and right to tell Mary and her husband what was going on. They were left puzzled and wondering what went wrong. She went back to the main house and when she went in she asked Mary and Gregory to sit down as it was time for them to know the truth. She began by apologising for running out of the house. The couple sat but speechless and with lots of questions flooding both their thoughts. They were just talking with eye signs wondering what now? But gave her an audience as requested.

Mosa started by introducing herself again. She said: my name is Mosa Grace Leuba Bogosi. Mary had not grasped the point and asked what Mosa's name had to do with the tantrum she threw earlier. She asked her why she threw the guest list on the floor and ran out. Gregory caught on fast and asked; wait a minute, did you just say Leuba, Bogosi? Yes. Mosa replied. He was at that moment holding a guest list and asked again; Bogosi as in Richard Bogosi? Mosa sighed and said: yes, I am Richard Bogosi's wife, no ex-wife. Mary jumped out of the chair in shock and said; what? How? Really? Gregory ordered her to calm down and sit down. He turned to Mosa and said how? I have known that guy for many years and I did not know if he was married. He never ever wore a wedding band let alone speak of a wife. Mosa asked the couple to calm down as she was willing to explain everything to them. She asked them to give her time to tell them a story of how she ended up been their domestic worker. Mary and Gregory were very shocked at that unexpected revelation. Mary just said I would really like to hear how the woman who used to be my maid is now a music star and now she is related to one of our biggest rivals in the industry. She continued and said; I knew there was something peculiar about you. Gregory asked his wife to give Mosa a chance to explain and he told her to begin explaining as they gave her the attention. Mary was just shocked at the fact that she hired a maid who was so prominent but yet modest to the fact that she was learned and holding an administration diploma.

Mosa started by telling them how she and Richard met. She further explained how they both loved music, how they used to sing together and how Richard was the best keyboardist at that time. She explained how they ended up getting married and about their first move to

Bluenburg. They also heard about their move to Richetown. She told them how she watched Richard grow in the music industry while she was seated at home with her dreams of becoming a singer dying a slow, painful death. She told them about the abuse, how it started and how it ended with Richard caging her in the house. How he forbade her from socialising, how he kept her away from family and friends and how he ended hiring the driver to buy groceries for their house, how when she was sick the doctor would be called to their house, she had all her beauty treatments done inside that same house. She told them how she was stopped from taking her children to school because she was talking to the principal about her husband abusing her. She continued until Mary was crying and shouting; Stop! Wait a minute. Are you telling us that Richard had you and the children locked up all the time? Yes. In this same suburb? Mary asked! We used to stay at number 789 Milkeyway avenue. I hope he still stays there. We have two boys and two girls. Ha! Marry clapped in shock. But Mosa said to them that the best was yet to come. She told them about the night Richard kicked them out to the streets while it was raining. How the next morning he ordered her to lick his shoes. Mary just asked her to please stop because the story was too painful to hear. She told them that she was about to finish as she had to tell them how she ended homeless and working as a domestic worker. She continued to tell them about the court and all that Richard did to her then and she arrived to a point where she was staying with Pule and his wife who got her the first domestic job at which she met Mary and ended staying in their back room. They were left with sympathy for all Mosa went through. She explained to them that she held her identity a secret because she wanted to move on with her life. She also wanted them to know that Richard might cause havoc at the album launch as they haven't met since the encounter at court.

Gregory immediately started planning protective measures to ensure that the whole night became Richard proof. He hired security men and gave them a picture of Richard, he also told them to make sure Mosa was always protected. The truth was they had to invite him to the event as he used to always invite them to his company events. Mosa agreed and also said that maybe he might not even cause a scene. Gregory and Mary hugged Mosa and promised her that all was going to be fine. They told her that she had all their support. For the first time in months Mosa felt some relieve after talking about all her pain to someone, she felt as though a weight had been lifted from her shoulders and all she was left with was to show her face to the world and sing her Praise which had been silenced for a very long time.

The day of the launch of Mosa's album arrived. It was a big because it was going live on a few television screens. The whole world was anticipating the big reveal of the face behind the praise song which had been heard around the world. The launch party was on everybody's lips and for that day Gregory worked really hard to make sure that everything was in order. Mary's job was to stay close to Mosa and keep her calm before she could ascend the stage. Gregory had to drive them very early that morning to the venue and they spent the day in the back room at the venue. They were avoiding the chance that someone would see them before the big reveal. They spent the whole day locked up in the backroom at the venue until the event started. The media was going crazy interrogating everybody connected to G.M music but unfortunately no one knew who the mysterious praise singer was. People came in thousand to the stadium where the event was. Tickets had been sold out and Gregory just saw the event doing exactly what was expected. He saw the rise of his company from the ashes to great victory and all was thanks to the voice of an angel called Mosa. As Mary knew a lot about hair and makeup, she turned Mosa into the most beautiful woman for that day. They had a beautiful dress designed just for her, a perfect fit and because she a beautifully shaped body, a curvaceous size thirty six, with a waist well shaped one would never believe she gave birth to four children. On that day she would walk down the streets and men were going to fall on their faces trying to get her. Only a stupid man like Richard would not appreciate such beauty. She looked so perfect for that day not even her past was going to ruin her joy. Mary also looked so glamorous, that was really a prestigious event.

The plan was to first reveal the CD cover as a big poster and then after a big announcement Mosa was to come out of that poster and reveal her face to the world. The moment of truth arrived as the people took their seats, even Richard arrived with his friends and a little pretty lady hanging on his arm. As usual he was proudly parading as a peacock. Gregory was watching him as he went past and simply greeted him. He and his friends sat down and after the programme director introduced Gregory and the people listened attentively but he kept the suspense by reading the line-up of singers who were going to perform that day.

The festival went on with musicians singing their lungs out and crowds happy, dancing, whistling, screaming and shouting for joy. It really was a joyous event. Gregory was so nervous because the investors were there and watching every movement. Of all the people who were there they seemed to be the only serious group. Whenever he looked at them he shivered with fear. The big moment arrived when the last singer gave a last performance. The crowed clapped as Gregory got called back to the stage. He continued from where he stopped with his speech. He kept the suspense going by thanking everybody for coming but before he could finish his sentence the crowds went wild and requested the revelation. The first revelation was the CD cover on a huge poster. On it was Mosa's face and the name of the album was written, I Praise God. The picture looked so beautiful and Richard immediately recognised the face of his ex-wife. He became very uncomfortable but tried to hide it. Gregory calmed the crowds as they were wild with joy, they were screaming uncontrollably and everything was live on television. The stadium was filled with joy, it was as if the people were welcoming the New Year. Because Mosa's name was purposely left out of the poster Gregory had the pleasure of announcing the star of the day. It was the greatest moment when he announced saying: Ladies And Gentlemen, Our beautiful audience around the world I urge you to give a big round of applause to MOSA, GRACE LEUBA!!!!!! The poster tore and Mosa came out running. She looked exquisite. Her big moment arrived. She was given a microphone to sing but Gregory signalled her to introduce herself. She took it, opened her mouth and said: Hello Everybody! My name is Mosa Grace Leuba, this is my praise, and I am going to sing it to God and to you. No one can take it away from me! She released the most beautiful, angelic voice. The stadium was so quiet you could hear a mouse running. All they were giving attention to was Mosa Leuba. She sang two songs and when she was done everybody in that stadium stood and clapped like crazy even the investors stood smiling and clapping, some of them were even knotting their heads with approval. Gregory just hugged his wife and said to her; we did it! They were so happy. Down at the VIP section something happened. The moment Gregory made the announcement Richard stood on his feet and mistakenly screamed: that's my wife as he was clapping hands. His friends looked at him with shock in their faces, he sat down feeling as embarrassed as if fart just blew from behind him promptly. One of his friends confronted him and asked him: did you just say that was your wife? How? Why did you not tell us? Did you know she could sing that well? Why did you not record her yourself? He kept answering yes, no and I don't know. The girl who was his date asked him: is it a yes or a no or you don't know? What exactly is it? He was so full of shame he ran off to his car. He locked himself in his car and stayed there for a very long time. He was sweating, shaking like he just saw a ghost. He kept asking lots of questions in his mind. How did Mosa end singing for his rival record company. How he was going to prevent the media from writing about their connection? How he was going to come out of all that?

The event came to an end with everybody congratulating Gregory on a successful night. Mosa was the star she always dreamed to be. There was no turning back after that night, her life was changed for the best. They waited for the crowds to clear and for everything to be properly packed up before they could leave the venue. Gregory, Mary, Mosa, Pule, Ouma and Rose left at dawn and as they were walking to the car with all the guards around them. They were busy discussing the rays of the sun and the weather. They saw something strange at the car park. People who were at that concert had left that place for about two hours by then. There was one car and Mosa recognised that it belonged to Richard. He immediately came out of the car as he saw them approached. The guards tried to stop him from coming closer but Mosa stopped them, she asked him what he wanted. He said congratulations to Mosa and she thanked him. He tried to continue talking but Gregory interrupted him and told him Mosa was up all night and she needed to go home and rest. He also told Richard to go home and do the same. They left him standing there as they went home and slept for most of the following day because Gregory ordered Mosa and Mary to switch their cell phones off to avoid the media pestering them. That whole Saturday they slept and only woke up to have dinner. While they were eating dinner they switched their cell phones on and Richard had somehow gotten hold of Mosa's new number and he had left twenty four voice messages on her phone. All the messages were saying that he wanted to see her. Mosa realised that Richard was desperate, how else would you explain anybody sane leaving twenty four messages.

They ate while Gregory was reading all the newspaper headlines about Mosa. Every newspaper had her beautiful face splashed all over it, she was the news on everyone's lips. Everybody went to bed that Saturday night very happy but the people who were more grateful were Mary and Gregory. Their company was just saved by grace, literally. The next morning they woke up to a door bell ringing nonstop. Mary thought it was Lizzie because she always woke her up with or for news. In that case they were expecting her to cause them chaos because Mary kept the fact of their maid been a musician away from her. She was known to always make a mountain out of a molehill. Mary opened the door and she was surprised to see Richard at their front door. He greeted and Mary greeted him back she asked him what he wanted that early in the morning. He said he wanted Mosa's address. Mary rushed back to the bedroom to wake her husband up but met him on his way out. He heard the noise caused by his wife and Richard. At the back room Mosa and her sister woke up and while Gregory and Mary were busy trying to chase Richard away Mosa and Rose walked in to check what the noise was all about.

She walked in and asked Richard what he was doing there. She was shocked to see him that very early in the morning like he sold newspapers. He said he wanted to talk to Mosa privately. Mosa said to Mary that she wanted to hear what he had to say. Rose was very angry, she told her sister to throw him out. Mary allowed him to come into the house but her husband and Rose remained in the room. Richard repeated to ask Mosa to talk to her privately. Mosa signalled her sister and Gregory using her eyes to please leave the room. They left but Gregory said to her: we are in the next room, any wrong move he makes, shout and we will call the police. He pointed a finger at Richard and said; remember you are trespassing. Richard and Mosa were now left alone in the room when he started by congratulating her and she thanked him. Mosa asked him again and said: Richard how can I help you again. At that time Mary was listening in through a slightly opened door. Her husband tried to stop her but she told her she doesn't trust Richard.

The conversation between Mosa and Richard went like this.

Richard: so you live here?

Mosa: Yes, no, kind off

Richard: yes, no, kind off, what is it exactly?

Mosa: yes I live here, why do you ask?

Richard: oh! So how do you know them?

Mosa: I used to be their maid.

Richard: maid? What? When?

Mosa: are you really surprised?

Richard: yes!

Mosa: HEHE! (Mosa clapped and laughed aloud)

Mosa: after what you put me through, you should not be surprised at me been a maid.

Richard: I am sorry, the real reason I came here was to apologise.

Mosa: apologise? Really? Ha!

Richard: look here, I am so sorry about how things worked out between us.

Mosa: apology accepted. Now please leave, it is too early for all this drama,

Richard: so they were your bosses before? How did that happen?

Mosa: Richard please leave, I told you it is too early in the morning. Besides I told you it was none of your business, now get out and leave me alone, please.

Richard: oh! So you are throwing me out?

Mosa: you mean like you threw me and our children out of your house on a rainy day? No this is not my house, besides you said you came to apologise and I forgave you, now leave.

Richard: I actually wanted to ask you how it felt to be famous, you are now a celebrity, and your name and face are all over the media, how does it feel?

Mosa: Hey! You lost the right to ask me how I felt a long time ago when you chased me out of your house. Oh no! Maybe it was when you tricked me and called me all the way from Stoneville to humiliate and divorced me.

Richard: I actually wanted to ask you for a favour.

Mosa: A favour? What favour? As far as you know, do I owe you any?

Richard: I wanted to ask you to keep our marriage and divorce news out of the media. I don't want people to know our private business.

Mosa: oh! So you wanted me to keep the fact that you held me prisoner in your mansion under the pretence of marriage for fourteen years and how you threw me and your undressed children out in the rain at night to make space for your new found conquest.

Richard: no……..

Mosa: oh! Wait a minute, I know; how about the fact that you bribed you friend at court and robbed me of everything, how you squeezed me into a corner and forced to sign the fraudulent divorce papers knowing very well that you were stealing from me and leaving with the responsibility of taking care of four children, penniless.

Richard: No, listen.

Mosa: oh! Oh! I know, how about if I showed them the most expensive shoes you gave me after kicking them in my face and breaking my nose.

Richard tried to hold Mosa's hand when she shouted: leave me alone! Don't touch me! You are here because you are afraid that people will know how heartless and cruel you have been to me and your children. Don't worry they will investigate and find the truth out without my assistance, I won't stop them. How foolish I was to think that you genuinely came to apologise. You made me believe I have your support but you did not care nor have a vein of remorse in bloodstreams. When Richard saw that he was caught out he tried to get Mosa to lower her voice but things were already heating up. Mosa shouted and said: you think I care that people will hear that you are a heartless monster? They know everything you did to me, you evil man. I already told them.

Richard: what? Why did you tell them? It's none of their business

Mosa: why? Why? They had the right to know who I was and all I have been through, since they gave me a roof over my head, provided me with food and money which enables me to carry the burden of four children you left for me to fend for. They are a reason you dragged yourself here today. They realised what you had forgotten about me and made me. If it wasn't for them the children of your loins would be starving to death like they were fatherless while you are living a high life like a single person in this town. So they have every right to know who and what you did to me. Now leave! Before I call the police.

As Mosa was shouting, Gregory, Mary and Rose came out of the other room and were looking straight at Richard. He felt embarrassed for causing noise in their house so he told them he was just leaving. Before he went out the door Mosa stopped him and said to him: Richard! You took away my dignity and joy, robbed me off my dream to sing gospel, made me believe I was worthless, and humiliated me to a point where I felt ugly just because you reminded me of how poor and ugly I was. You called me so many names I nearly forgot who I was. You cursed and shamed me every chance you got. You turned me into your punching bag and your baby making machine. You broke my confidence and tormented me into believing I was useless and could not do anything without you. I suffered at your hand just to bring your dream of producing to life. You grew and left me down below as if you forgot that I held an administration diploma. I nearly forgot how to praise and worship because you made me. I endured pain and hardships from you, the love of my life and the only man I knew and dedicated myself to. She wiped a tear from her eye and said: Your mission in life was to destroy me. You forgot your promises to me but you did not take my voice away. The one and only thing that brought us together. The same thing that turned you from a loving, kind and God fearing man, into a devil possessed monster. Praise and worship. YOU COULD NOT TAKE THAT AWAY FROM ME. Richard did not respond instead he left so embarrassed by all that happened.

Thirteen

Live carried on smoothly for Mosa after she became a household name. Her music sold like hot potatoes at the corner café. In six months' time after the album launch, Mary and Gregory's company became so big in the music industry all thanks to Mosa and her brilliant voice. She had enough money to buy a house and a car but her granny advised her against uprooting the children from Stoneville. She wanted to avoid frustrating them that soon after they had to leave their house. They were settling in Stoneville and Mmaleuba thought that Mosa can visit them and vice versa during the school holidays. For the first time in many years Mosa was very confident, she was happy to even form a group where she was counselling women. She was helping the less fortunate and even became a mentor to young and upcoming musicians. When counselling people she referred to her experiences whenever need arose. People from around the world respected her and that made her ex-husband feel more foolish for everything he did to her.

With Richard things did not go as well as they used to. Because he treated people badly he ended losing all his money at the hand of his angry accountant who disappeared with everything he owned. The devastating truth hit Richard like a ton of bricks when he realised that he had not a cent to his name plus his company was going to suffer because he did not make an effort to appreciate the hard work from his accountant instead he treated him like dirt. The accountant flee from the country without warning and vacated his offices. Richard and all his other clients laid a charge against him but they were told it was going to be very difficult to trace a fugitive. He left Richard in a mess with the bond payment, revenue services and a whole lot of debts.

It took Richard two years before he could give up. For that period of time he begged and borrowed with the hope that by any chance his accountant would resurface with his money and rescue him. When that seemed to be taking too long he sold shares in his company again with the hope to save his employees but all ended in him finding himself in a hostile takeover. His newfound partner turned on him and stole the company from under his nose. Richard was left destitute so he resorted to selling his cars and house to pay off his debts. Within a few months he was left jobless, penniless and homeless. Like they say in the world: KARMA is a ....! All his friend forsook him and not to mention his groupies. He was left living in his car while he was trying to at least find a job. People who knew him as high and mighty mocked him and laughed at him whenever he asked them for help. His life took a three hundred and sixty degree turn for the worst. When all this was happening he was busy keeping track of his ex-wife's flourishing career. Guilt and shame were also taking their pieces out of him. He lost everything like a prodigal son and likewise he decided it was time for him to swallow his pride and return home to his parent's house in Bridgeville where his sister, husband and children lived. He shamefully begged them for shelter and narrated his story to them. His sister and her husband welcomed him with opened arms, his brother in law promised to help him look for work. He asked them to accompany him as he went to apologise to his aunt and uncles for his bad behaviour. The family members forgave him but his uncle who was a pastor advised him to return to God and beg him for forgiveness.

That same Sunday Richard went to church after a long time. He prayed God and asked for forgiveness. After church he went to counselling and there he told the brother who was helping him how he felt about his past life. He confessed and to the counsellor's surprise he even broke into tears. The man advised him to go and apologise to his wife and children. He responded by saying it was not going to be easy as his wife wanted nothing to do with him. They prayed and the man told him to trust God. He started a search for work and it was not easy. He could find a short contract here and there but it was not enough. He really seemed to be punished for his sins. In the meantime he asked the permission to play keyboard at church, which was granted. That revived his music passion he even felt the need to start teaching children how to play music instruments. The pastor allowed him to conduct music classes at church and they became very successful and that brought great comfort to him. All this was God taking him back to his old humble self. It was as if he went to visit the young, humble, respectful and caring Richard again. It was as if he was at a time of revival where he was reminded of who and how he was, not only that but it was the restoration process he had to go through.

The time came where the pastor and his family members had to accompany him to Stoneville where he had to go and apologise to his wife, her family and children. That was the most difficult of all the challenges he went through because those were the people he hurt the most. He asked Mmamoruti to arrange everything and as it was done in cultural believes Richard and Mosa were not divorced because the dowry was still in the possession of the Leuba family even though he gave her four children but because he abounded his children it was considered a time out for the two. The elders were aiming at reconciliation between the two. Richard was hopeless even after all he went through trying to transform into a new person. Mmaleuba had no choice but to respect her in-laws. She called Mosa and told her about the meeting request from the Bogosi family. Mosa nearly fainted because she knew it meant trouble had just started. She had to face the demons which were avoided for a very long time. Her heart pounded like a hammer, sweat ran on her face like she just saw Richard next to her. She replied her granny with a shivering voice telling her to arrange the meeting and promised to arrive home the day before.

Mosa fell into a depression mode, from that day she kept wondering what the next Saturday was bringing. She knew how the elders could dictate situations, especially marriages. In her case it was either she was to be forced to reunite with her husband or she was going to be forced to share custody with a man who rejected his own children. She came up with a plan of action. She called her sister and asked her to prepare the papers from their divorce. She also asked her sister to prepare the surprise box. Before they could think about anything Mosa arrived for the meeting two days ahead. She told her granny how she came to help them prepare as that was a big meeting.

The day of the meeting arrived and all Mosa's uncles arrived two hours early to discuss what their in-laws could be looking for as it was three years since Mosa had left her matrimonial home and they said nor did nothing until then. As elders tend to exaggerate things the uncles were worried that they wanted to cash in on Mosa's share of music riches. They strategized on how they were going to handle the meeting while Mmaleuba and Mosa were told to keep quiet unless if requested to speak.

The Bogosi family arrived with Richard as humble as a wet cock. His head was bowed so low snot would have a freeway to the floor from his nose. When Mosa saw him she started to boil with anger but her granny calmed her by holding hands. The meeting continued with both sides apologising for all that happened in the past. The talks reached a hilltop when Richard requested to see his children. Mosa burst into tears and angrily asked; whose children are you asking to see? Ha? One of her uncles ordered her to be quiet and allow them to handle the matter. Richard apologised and told them he actually wanted to apologise to the children for how he treated them and their mother. Mosa was busy biting her tongue blood was about to splash out any minute. The uncles ordered Rose to bring Mosa's children and the minute they arrived Richard got on his knees. He apologised to his children with tears rolling from his eyes. It was such a heartfelt apology that made everybody present emotional. The children stood there motionless as if they were told by somebody to remain silent. Rose took them in and the meeting continued Richard turning on his wife and continuing with his emotional plead for forgiveness. History flooded Mosa's mind and when she remembered how Richard bowed and apologised the same way after nearly killing her. Tears rolled from her eyes and she could not stop crying so she stormed out and was followed by one of her aunts, who locked the room and spoke to her. She calmed her and spoke to her and begged her to forgive her husband. She sold her the piece where Richard had been punished by God for all he did to them. Mosa's aunt reminded her why she should forgive her husband and really begged on Richard's behalf. It was a long and not so easy conversation but at the ultimate end Mosa came out of the house with her aunt holding her hand for support as she requested an audience. The elders were busy talking but abandoned their topic and gave the deserved attention to her.

Mosa started by apologising for a disrespectful manner in which she stormed out of the meeting. She further apologised to Richard for not giving him a chance to speak. She sat down and started from the beginning where she told everybody the story that lead to them meeting. The details of all her story melted even the hardest heart. The elders were weeping, Mmaleuba was the only calm one as she opened a box and took out Richard's most expensive shoes out and Mosa narrated the story about the blood stained shoes. She presented her last evidence in a form of a brown envelope. It was the divorce decree accompanied by all the documents stating that Richards takes all of their possessions except the children. They read the papers just before Mosa could ask them in a very polite manner saying: now, can anyone of you ever take someone who treated them in the way this man treated me? The uncles and the aunts remained very quiet as Mosa continued asking them many question about what will happen if he changes again. Richard jumped in and bowed before her saying: I promise baby, I will never, ever be like that again. She ignored him and said to the elders: we have been here before and he made the same promises he is making now. I can't put my children through that trauma again. I am sorry my elders, but you have wasted a trip. I have forgiven Richard, but I don't want to reunite with him. He fraudulently divorced me, now as the saying goes; "he made his bed, let him lye in it" the elders where helpless but Richard quickly got an idea and asked for a chance to present it. He was offered the chance and he took a deep breath and said: My wife I am very sorry for what I put you and our children through, I know it will be difficult to accept me back easily. So I beg you to give me a last chance. I won't ask to uproot your lives again and take you to Richetown, but because I have lost everything I beg you to give me at least three months to show you how I have changed. If in that timeframe I do something or show a sign that reflects my past behaviour then don't ever take me back as your husband. He continued and said but if the three month passes and I have shown no sign of being abusive or impulsive or arrogant for that matter, please promise me that you will marry me again. I know I wronged you. I caged you in our house, I cursed you and did inhuman things to you but for the love of God I beg you, please forgive me. It took a punishment from above to wake me up from the slumber I was in. I have realised what kind of a monster I had become and I am very remorseful about all that, I am in the process of rejuvenation and I swear the devil that possessed me before will never get the better of me again. He pleaded his case and his speech melted Mosa's heart. She picked him up from the floor and told him she will reconsider a reunion after three months. All the elders from both the families sighed a sigh of relieve that at the end of such a long meeting there was hope. It was clear that reconciliation was in the plans of both the families by how they celebrated after Mosa said she would give Richard a chance to prove he had changed.

The meeting ended on a high note when the Bogosi family left that night. All his elders promised to support him and help him through his challenges while trying to win his wife and children back. After everybody left Mmaleuba tried to check if Mosa really meant what she said by promising to take Richard back after three months if he has changed. Mosa told her granny she was not ready to discuss anything until three months from that day. On their way back Richard told his family how happy he was that his wife was willing to give him a chance to prove himself. He prayed to God to give him strength to go through it all.

The three months started by Richard doing what he had done in a very long time. He called the Leuba house the next morning and asked to speak to all his children. Mosa was very surprised but kept a room for disappointment and asked her granny to monitor how long it was going to last. It was on a Sunday and Mosa left for Richtown but just before she left Richard called her and wished her a safe journey back. She was pleased but managed to hide it from him. He continued with his good behaviour and with all he was doing in church until he received news from an old friend and partner who visited him from overseas and received the bad news.

He called Richard and asked him to meet in Richetown. Because Richard was broke he had no money to fill his petrol tank for his trip, so he told his friend who transferred money for him to be able to make it to Richetown.

Upon his arrival in Richetown he had no choice but to ask for accommodation from his ex-wife while he was meeting a friend. Mosa agreed to have him stay over at her house but prepared a spare room for him. They were very cold towards each other in the beginning but ended catching up, laughing and very cosy. Mosa quickly jumped from a compromising position and left Richard embarrassed on the couch. From there onwards they became very awkward towards each other.

The next morning Richard left to meet his friend who invited him on a free trip abroad but Richard rejected the offer. His friend was surprised because he knew Richard to be a very impulsive man who was irresponsible and would have jumped at an offer of a free plane ticket, but that time he was refusing to travel. He was very close to Richard and knew him very well. Richard told him all that happened to him to a point where he had nothing. He felt sorry for Richard and offered to help only if he was supplied with proof of Richard been robbed of his business. He was a big man and was very famous and people in South Africa remembered him from the time when he used to work with Richard. He visited Richard at Mosa's house and told her about the trip Richard just rejected unknowingly to him Mosa was really impressed. She was slowly recognising bits and pieces of change in her ex-husband. The name of Richard's friend was Brian and his first alphabet was the B in RB records which was their company before he sold his shares for greener pastures abroad. He promised Richard to help him get his company back before he went abroad.

Brian was very connected and immediately after hearing about the bad luck that fell on his friend he started phoning people from around the world and asked them to trace the whereabouts of the accountant. He also called in some favours in digging up information on the people who stole his best friend's company. He ate dinner with Richard and his wife and while they were busy eating dessert he asked to be excused as he had somewhere to rush off to. They were left wondering where he could be running to. He left to meet someone who had traced the accountant. After dinner Richard told Mosa that he was preparing for his trip back to Bridgeville on Saturday morning. The woman was not keen on him returning home but pretended she was fine with Richard leaving. They went to bed but what was surprising was Richard receiving a bank notification message which reported a huge lump sum of money into his bank account. He woke up in the morning and told Mosa that he had to rush to the bank. Mosa asked why and he told her it might be great news for him, he told her that all will be revealed when he got back from the bank. While they were talking a call came in from Brian who asked him to meet. He was puzzled as to why Brian wanted to meet. He rushed off to the bank and when he got there the manager told him the money belonged to him and was transferred in the middle of the night. When Richard asked from which account he recognised the initials to be those of his former accountant. He was so happy he just bowed and lifted his hands and said: "thank you my Father".

He went and met with Brian who also came with great news. He told her that he was the one who traced the accountant and made sure he transferred the money into his account. Before Richard could thank him, he stopped Richard and told him that he has bought back RB records back. He used his money to buy the company and told Richard how he had to pay him back. He told Richard to start taking over his company by tomorrow which was a Friday. Richard felt as if he was dreaming and he would wake up and find all that to be unreal. All was very real and Richard was not dreaming. God had put him through all that because he did not appreciate his family. He took him back to where he began to remind him of what was important. After all Richard had gone through he was truly remorseful and the Grace of God returned all that the devil who used him to abuse his wife and children stole from him. He visited Richetown on Sunday to meet his long lost best friend but by Wednesday afternoon he had all that belonged to him returned miraculously at the hand of his best friend. Brian tried to buy the most expensive Champaign to celebrate as they normally did, but Richard rejected and told him he does not drink anymore and he intend to keep it that way forever. He told him about the challenge he was facing to win back the love of his wife back. Brian advised him on what to do.

Richard rushed back to Mosa's house. He arrived and found Mosa still at work. He gave the house helper the night off and started cooking a romantic dinner for him and Mosa. When Mosa arrived she was surprised to find Richard in an apron and asked him what he was doing in the kitchen. In the years they were married Richard never cooked, even when Mosa was sick he would rather buy take away food. Mosa was rightfully amazed by seeing him in the kitchen. He pulled the chair for her and told him to sit while he was pouring some juice for her. Before he could give her food he told her all that happened to lift his mood. She was so happy for him, she jumped from the chair and thanked God for his grace. Because the old feelings were busy revived by the few days they spent together, Mosa hugged Richard with a long and warm embrace. When they tried to let go of each other they kissed and they don't know how it happened but that night became the night of reconciliation, the passion returned to a couple who separated for almost over four years. That night dinner was left to be cold and Richard took his rightful place next to his wife in the main bedroom. He and his wife reconciled and all was forgiven and forgotten. The next morning

Richard asked his ex-wife to remarry him. Their anniversary was approaching and he proposed that they should revive their marriage on the same day they were officially married. Because she was on cloud nine Mosa agreed to everything her husband suggested.

Richard was given three months to convince his wife to take him back but fate brought them back together only halfway through the deadline. Mosa was a bit sceptical and asked Richard if they could keep their reunion a secret just for a while until they are sure about how they truly felt but he knew that there was no way out as all he wanted was a chance to be an honest husband to his wife and a father to his children. Richard was disappointed but because he understood where Mosa came from he agreed. The Friday morning came with great change for Richard and Mosa because to prove that he changed he asked a lawyer to draw papers sharing fifty percent of his company to her as he believed the children were still under eighteen, they had a clause added which stipulated there to be a share for them. She was shocked but accepted the offer. They walked in the recording studios hand in hand to take over as partners. A month came to an end and they drove to Stoneville in one car to visit the children. It was September holidays so they were going to pick the children up for a visit to Richetown. As soon as they jumped off the car Mmaleuba saw a glow in Mosa that she saw on her when she came back from the Bluenburg conference. She immediately realised that even if they were trying to hide it, the two had reconciled. She was happy but also tried very hard to hide it. That night Mosa prepared a spare room for Richard as they had to keep up the pretence. They left the next morning, unknowingly to Mosa Richard had booked them on a trip to Zenji, for them to have a second honeymoon but this time as a family of six. They went a day after their arrival in Richetown.

After the holidays the couple confirmed their reunion to their families and even informed them about a wedding ceremony they were planning. They called it the revival of their wedding vows. They were closer than ever. They loved each other very much. Shared an office and did everything together like going to church, meetings and even shopping. Richard was determined to avoid all his first mistakes at all cost. Everything got revived in their marriage even the intimacy level raised to the highest level. Richard Bogosi became a complete new man who appreciated his wife and children more than ever. His first born son became closer to him and he was happy to see his father as a good example in his life. He matured and became an example to married people who asked for marital advice from him and his wife. They always answered by telling the couples about five fundamental principles of a successful marriage, which are: Love, Prayer, Patience, Respect and most of all true Forgiveness. The most important advice they gave to people was to befriend themselves with the word of God as all the answers were coming from it. They would always quote scriptures like Proverbs 3 v 5 and 6(NKJV) which says "Trust in the Lord with all your heart and lean not on your own understanding. In all your ways acknowledge him and he shall direct your path". They always told people how Richard got lost along his Christian journey to the sinful nature which he went to because he lost his way and trust in the Lord. Grace was always convicted to teach young and old women about forgiveness and how in the end it brings fruit to one's life. She always encouraged couples to fast and pray for one another and to forget about competing with other people as God was and is the giver of life and all the blessings in it. She always strengthened those who came to her for advice with prayers and the word of God which kept her growing from one level of glory to another. TO GOD BE THE GLORY FOR ALL THE GREAT THINGS HE HAS DONE.